Bill Karlson, CPC

In the next twelve months one in five people will suddenly lose their job. Bill Karlson takes the trauma out of career change, helps you find your life's passion and shows you how to get top dollars in a job you love.

THIRD EDITION

THIRD EDITION

World Career Achievement Company
Franklin, Tennessee

Publisher's Cataloging-in-Publication
(Provided by Quality Books, Inc.)

Karlson, Bill.
    Get top $$$ in a job you love! / Bill Karlson. -- 3rd ed.
    p. cm.
    Includes index.
    Preassigned LCCN: 97-60432
    ISBN: 1-887689-17-6

    1. Career development.   2. Job hunting.
    I. Title. II. Title:
    Get top dollars in a job you love!

HF5381.K37 2002   650.1'4
                        QBI97-40377

We have been careful to provide accurate information throughout this book, but it is possible that errors and omissions have been introduced. Please consider this in making any career plans or other important decisions. Trust your own judgement above all else and in all things.

GET TOP $$$ IN A JOB YOU LOVE!

This book equips you *with a set of tools* to:

- become very clear about your career direction
- really understand the job search process
- get hired at top starting salary!

Are you

- unclear about career direction?
- baffled by the job search process?
- lost as to how and why people *really* get hired?

DO NOT immediately prepare a résumé.
DO NOT immediately try to network by
calling friends and contacts for job leads.

Dedication

I don't believe I can achieve much of value in my life without significant help.

This book is dedicated to the many people in my life who have made my dream of sharing what I have learned about living a passionate life come true.

This includes my supportive father, Pop, and terrific wife, Myra. My professional development and support team is invaluable: Mac and Cheryl McClure, Rex Mitchell, Chris Heftel, Sherry Pride, Cindy Head and the hundreds of individuals who continue to let me know how this program works. Thanks to Ron Bell for the terrific artwork. Most of all, I dedicate this work and the rest of my life to God.

Mile 00

It's time for the *career* trip of your life!

About the author

Bill Karlson, CPC

Over 20 years helping people get jobs
they can be *passionate* about.

Corporate Career Expertise
• 14 years management with Fortune 50 corporation
• Executive Recruiter at nation's largest search firm

Entrepreneurial Career Expertise
• Started own executive search firm
• Author, speaker and host of radio talk show

International Career Expertise
• Chief Operating Officer of international firm
• Director of Executive Search & Job Search Training

Why bother to read any further?

Because you want top dollars in a job you love! Are you looking for a better job with your present employer or a new job with another company? Do you know exactly which way to go? By investing your time in working through <u>Miles 01</u>-<u>12</u> and following through with the contacts necessary, you *can* achieve top dollars in a job you love.

Recently a person called to say that they had been fired and did not know what to do next. They were lost and demoralized. They faced severe financial problems within a few months. They followed the suggestions in this book. Within two days they had called thirty companies, arranged fifteen informational interviews and found three solid job openings. Their comment? "If someone had told me that I would have any chance at a new job within a few weeks I would have told them they were crazy! This program works!"

Finding a career you can get passionate about could be a painful experience for you, possibly the toughest challenge you've ever faced.

If it were up to you, you might not be taking a career trip at all. The old way of finding a new job includes the painful rejection caused by interviews, phone calls and letters with no response. You may end up riding the roller coaster of the five phase psychological cycle that people go through when experiencing extreme trauma. First comes denial, "This isn't happening." And then anger at the continuing rejection. This is where you may be now.

You'll try to bargain to make things work out your way, then experience deep sadness when they don't. Finally, you'll accept your situation and move ahead. You may be thinking, "I don't want to do this." Routine resistance has started, but let's move ahead.

What this book is really about

This book guides you through the job search maze. We'll equip you to choose a job that allows you to realize your dreams and be passionate in what you do.

The alternative? Life By Accidentsm jobs which have little to do with your true career destination. You may drift from one job to another searching for career fulfillment.

Our commitment to you

Our commitment to you includes updating this leading-edge book on how people are hired. Here are just a few of the areas constantly being revised: the most effective techniques in self-assessment, goal setting, career search, résumé preparation, professional interviewing skills and salary negotiation. *We know the secret of how people get hired.* We advise those who are first time job seekers, university graduates and trade school students. We also work closely with those that have been fired, laid-off, retired, white collar managers and corporate executives. We have helped military and government professionals who are faced with the difficulty of translating previous skills into reasons the private sector will hire them. We offer seminars, tapes and other support materials. Call (800) 259-7711 for information.

Your career goals

From this point forward, consider yourself a professional crafts person with a tool kit of skills. We will teach you to market these skills to those who are willing to pay for your full value. This book will give you several powerful benefits. Follow the specific directions and you will:

- know what motivates you and what you want to do – identify your personality;

- achieve a clear career path, including the steps needed to reach your next job;

- translate previous successes into a future oriented *Advantage-Driven Résumé*sm;

- feel good about the *Advantages* you have to offer;

- locate employers with jobs that match your *Advantages;*

- seek the top starting salary in a job you can be passionate about; and

- use references to professionally support getting your job.

When individuals focus on their abilities and their dreams, they get inspired to fulfill their career and personal goals: we call this *career passion*. Employers search for this characteristic. When a hiring authority is trying to decide between two candidates and you have a passion for the job they want to fill, this one attribute could sway their decision your way.

Your commitment

This program can improve your life as well as your career. Make a strong commitment to apply what you learn in each Mile and you are on your way to success. This is not the time to ask for input from your spouse, family, or friends. Give yourself this opportunity to deeply think through what *you* really want. Later, if appropriate, get input from those you respect. Review each Mile thoroughly before continuing to the next.

Welcome to the first Mile on the road to the career of your dreams!

Mile 01 of your career road trip begins with this overview.

At Mile 02, define the type of work environment that suits you best. Have you chosen a career path that is heading in the wrong direction? No more wrong turns please!

At Mile 03, we introduce you to a new concept in selecting a job or a new career. We present information in a way that quickly matches your skills with an employer's needs. You pack *Items* and *Successes* to take with you on your career trip. This detailed job and life experience history identifies what you have to offer in the future, rather than what you've done previously.

As you cruise through Mile 04, you'll prioritize your life goals. You'll determine goals in eight categories of your life and make plans for their achievement. Goal prioritization is one of the most powerful parts of this program. Your mind must be focused and organized to function properly. Consistently updating and prioritizing your goals will significantly improve your life. Without a clear destination you will probably get lost.

It's important to take the time to examine what you expect from life and your next job. For example, minimizing travel may affect your career options.

At Mile 05, you'll consider your ideal career and next job destination (the career path you are most passionate about). You'll consider the kind of organization you'd like to work for, where you'd like to live, and what salary you'll need. It's a chance to go for the dream you've always had but never felt comfortable seriously examining.

While you're on a roll, Mile 06 asks you to choose other exciting career destinations and pick other career paths. Although you will have a first choice career option, prioritizing your goals may force you to take a second or third job option that's less than ideal. Careful analysis and planning to meet all of your goals really drive Miles 05 and 06.

Mile 07 is where your job search planning pays off. Researching organizations is a critical factor in finding the career of your dreams.

We'll discuss resources and show where to go to find the companies that need your skills. A trip to your library and getting on the Internet may be appropriate. You'll learn where to find professional recruiters who can help you secure a job in your field.

You'll pause to research companies that you'd like to work for. No more sending résumés to want ads or making calls to busy, unresponsive folk in human resources. You'll profile these companies by industry, ideal location, financial status, size and other factors *that match your goals.* You'll document contacts for initial presentation and later follow-up.

At <u>Mile 08</u>, you finally arrive where most people start when they begin a new career or a new job search, by updating their résumé. This time, you'll learn the secret to writing the world's most powerful résumé.

<u>Mile 09</u> defines *positive* networking techniques and maximizes your networking skills as you make the first contact with your ideal companies. We suggest who to call and what to say.

<u>Mile 10</u> begins your 50 markers-a-day plan, designed to track your activities and results day by day. As powerful as this program can be, if worked diligently, finding your dream job requires sustained effort. Make your financial reserves last. Apply the 50 markers-a-day plan to your career future.

You can bypass career road blocks by following a few basic rules. If you want to change jobs, don't resign until you have another job. Review our suggested resignation letter as a guide. If you're unemployed, act as if the cash you have will last a year, because it might have to!

The critical steps to getting your new job include making numerous *positive* networking presentation telephone calls. These are made to companies you have researched. You can follow up on advertised job vacancies (or ones you discover yourself), presenting yourself for the job and seeking telephone interviews. Next, you set face-to-face interview dates and times, arrange reference checks, follow-up and track results.

Mile 11 prepares you for the exciting and potentially stressful experience of interviewing and negotiating a top salary. After years of experience in successful professional recruiting, we know how and why people get hired and we can save you many heartaches.

This is where you can win *your* career race. During the stress of an interview, most people respond to a question like, "So tell me about yourself," with something from their previous job experience or education background. This is the way to minimize your chances of a new career and lose a great job offer! Don't let this to happen to you.

Next, the question of money invariably comes up. Most people have an arbitrary figure to give when asked, "How much money are you making and how much do you need?" In response, some people inflate their salary needs, assuming they will have to come down later. Others carefully detail their previous salary history on the application. Neither of these approaches will get you the best starting pay. Our professional approach allows you to discover the best money a new employer will offer, without ever giving a salary figure.

Mile 12 addresses how to use professional references to get the job you've always wanted. Prepare your references to make the best possible recommendations by using our unique approach.

So why would you take *this* kind of trip?

This book takes much of the pain out of looking for a job and enables you to choose from the great opportunities you'll soon develop. Your career success requires careful consideration of all twelve Miles; however, once you have reached the last Mile marker, you'll be motivated to plan other important areas of your future.

Everything you do as you progress through each Mile helps prepare you for your telephone and face-to-face interviews.

If you are not willing to invest your time and effort to complete all the directions thoroughly, you must reevaluate your desire to make a positive change in your career. You alone hold the keys to your destination.

There's no turning back in pursuing the career of your dreams. *Ask yourself this question:* **"If I won the $100 million lottery and decided I wanted to continue working, what would I do?"** Wouldn't it be something you loved? If that's not what you are doing now, why not?

Use this book to achieve a career you can be passionate about. *Let's get rolling on Mile 02.*

See *your* map to the future!

Most people are bright, capable, and willing to earn their living through gainful employment, *just like you.* However, very few people have invested the time, or have received the guidance necessary, to discover who they are before they found themselves out of work or unfulfilled in their current job.

Life By Accident ahead

Many people have lived what I call a Life By Accident℠ (or LBA℠) experience. With no real sense of direction they have drifted into and out of several different jobs. None of these jobs were particularly fulfilling, even if the person had the skill to be successful and was well compensated for their work.

A business sales executive came into my office after having been laid-off due to a merger. He had completed an outplacement program but was still looking for a new job. The outplacement firm had done a professional job in detailing the man's work history. He was about as uninspired as he could have

been about what had been written down on his résumé. After chatting for a few minutes, I asked him
what he would do with his life if he won the lottery
and eventually chose to return to meaningful work.
After a few minutes of reflection his response was
delightful. He brightened considerably. His posture
became erect and his voice became filled with enthu-
siasm as he described his love of wood working and
general construction. His new mental picture of success had him out of his three-piece suits and into a
work shirt, boots and pick-up truck! His skill and
passion for building and subcontracting had grown
over the years after the construction of several of his
personal homes.

After working through the suggestions in this
book, he is now happily in the process of contacting
large local builders. He has blended his previous
sales success with his love of construction to crystal-
lize a new career path that he can really enjoy for the
rest of his life.

I do not recommend completely changing careers. You lose all of the experience you have so
painfully gained. You also have to start over in proving yourself, typically at wages lower than your
previous job. As in our example, *a blending of your
real work passion coupled with previous job experience is the most rewarding way to go.* Later, I'll
show you how to accomplish this goal.

If you are looking for a job, you have our
sincere compassion for the exceptional challenge
you're facing. You could be one of many people in
the middle of their career with "golden handcuffs."
We define this as a person making money in a job
they really don't enjoy, but don't hate enough to
leave, so they've decided to stay in a boring job
waiting for retirement, which may be many years

away! You have a choice. If you will take the time to determine who you are and what you really want, you can find ways to make a job you don't like more meaningful, or find one that really gets you excited.

Rarely does a person choose a career or a job based solely on their personality. However, the closer match your job is to your personality type, the greater success you will have in that position. In my many years of executive recruiting, I have discovered that it is neither who you are, nor what you do, that allows you to arrive at your ideal career destination. It's a marriage of the two.

This book will help you plan for your ideal job and follow a dynamic career path. Examples in the Appendix will be noted with a page number. The first "Helpful Hint," starting with Mile 02, can be found on Appendix page 109.

Take a few minutes to think about your interpersonal skills on the job. Through the book we'll make suggestions for specific actions to take. *We suggest writing down your answers in a separate notebook that you'll eventually take along to your interviews for reference.* Let's start by having you answer the following questions.

My preferred style of operation in the workplace

At work, I see myself as the kind of person who...

What do I think it's like working with me?

Which reflects your personality?

When I take a break, I normally

      prefer company   recharge alone.

I express myself best through

      writing   talking.

In casual conversation, I discuss

      many different things   one topic.

I'm more interested in

      facts   theory.

I make my decisions based more on

      logic   intuition.

At work, I prefer making decisions

      on my own   in a group.

I prefer my work day to be

      scheduled   spontaneous.

I prefer things in my life to be

      stable   changing.

Review your answers and ask yourself whether knowing your personality better would have helped you avoid a past Life By Accident experience. "Would it?" In most cases the answer is, "Yes!" Write down your choices in your notebook.

How your personality fits into an employer's culture is a *major* factor in determining how long you will be satisfied in your job.

These choices reveal something about your work ethic, interpersonal skills and personality. For an in-depth understanding of your personality type, and how it affects your professional and personal life, we suggest the following books: *Please Understand Me: Character and Temperament Types,* by David Keirsey and Marilyn Bates and *Do What You Are: Discover the Perfect Career For You Through the Secrets of Personality Type,* Paul Tieger and Barbara Barron-Tieger.

Your answers to Mile 02 will become the basis for examining and selecting your next position.

Now that you have a better understanding of how you relate to others, ask yourself the following questions. Use this information to choose the environment you want to work in and ensure a successful career. *Your understanding of how you relate to others greatly affects your work* (Appendix page 109).

1. Do you prefer a manager who gives you specific direction or lets you work out your own solutions?
2. Regardless of a specific career path, what general work would you like to do during a typical week?
3. What type of environment would let you do your best work: indoors, outdoors, fast-paced, stable?

4. What organizational structure would you prefer: a large corporation, "Mom and Pop," start-up, consulting, military, government, etc.?
5. What type of relationship do you prefer with management?
6. What type of relationship do you prefer with your peers?
7. What is your natural style in supervising others? If you've had no supervisory experience, what do you think your style would be?
8. What opportunities and support do you require for continuing your professional or technical development?
9. What professional equipment do you need to perform your job efficiently?
10. What work environment (space or traffic flow etc.) allows you to be most productive?

Reflecting on your answers to the preceding questions will help you understand the who, what, and where of your ideal career or next job. These questions, and those in other Miles, will give you a better idea of what questions you must ask during informational interviews (in Mile 06) and interviews with the hiring authority (in Mile 11). Your future employer must be a match with who you are and your ideal work situation, before you can confidently accept a job offer and avoid another Life By Accident experience.

From the above questions and answers, list the five most important questions you must have answered before you could say "Yes!" to a great career opportunity (Appendix page 111).

REST STOP

Stop reading now and take five minutes to write two or three sentences which summarize who you are and what type of work environment you need to be most productive.

What you have to offer!

Begin to see yourself as a professional crafts person. Which of your skills do you plan to put in your "tool kit"? You will need to identify what your specific skills are before you set out on your new career. Here in <u>Mile 03</u>, we'll decide what you have to offer a new employer (your advantages, if you like).

A young woman requested my help in determining a career path for her that made sense. She had received a degree in marine biology, but quickly found she had no real passion for what the jobs she found entailed. After several Life By Accident job experiences she was really lost. She had tried multi-level marketing, executive recruiting and even managing a timber company in New Hampshire! None worked out for her financially or emotionally. We followed this book's directions and quickly developed an extensive list of *Items* and *Successes* that support *Advantages* an employer would pay for and she would thoroughly enjoy doing. Once we had the list completed, she was well on her way to a meaningful and long lasting career path.

To match your skills to a future employer's job specifications in a way that will compel them to call you for an interview, you will be equipped in <u>Mile 08</u> with an *Advantage-Driven Résumé*. An *Advantage* is what you can do well for a future employer. An *Advantage* statement is backed up by your *Successes* and *Items* during current and former employment. *Items* are facts – what you have done. *Successes* are goals achieved for previous employers - related to your *Items*. Here are a few samples from the author's own career path as a Career Achievement Speaker/Job Search Trainer. The *Advantage* to a future employer is in **bold**:

• **Will present an exciting and professional image to your audience.** Successful seminar speaker for New York job fair *(Success)*. Sponsored by CNBC. Recorded professional speaker *(Items)*.
• **Will bring exceptional communications and interpersonal skills to career achievement.** Author, *GET TOP $$$ IN A JOB YOU LOVE! (Success)*. Top Producer in the state engineering recruiting competition *(Success)*. Nationally Certified Personnel Consultant *(Item)*.
• **Can positively affect audiences to want to proceed with their own career achievement.** Planned and conducted successful technical education seminars for Fortune 500 companies *(Success)*. Strong audience response, exceptional interest generated *(Success)*.

This preview sets the stage for two exercises which will help you determine your specific life gifts and the *Items* and *Successes* which you will later use to support the *Advantages* in your résumé. Sample *Advantage-Driven Résumé* on Appendix page 126.

Exercise 1: Your life's gifts

Give yourself the chance to thoroughly enjoy your life by working in a job you love! World-renowned author, Barbara Sher, makes an excellent point: "What you **love** to do is where you are gifted." Ms. Sher's *Live the Life You Love* and *I Could Do Anything If I Only Knew What It Was* are books that can help you discover your unique gifts.

Stories of my life that make me feel good

One of the founders of modern career counseling, Dr. Bernard Haldane, shared his secret with me for discovering your specific gifts. I believe his formula is so powerful, and so critical to your personal and business life, that I want you to use it.

Going back as far as you can remember, summarize five stories, events or personal experiences, where you felt great, won an award, learned a very uplifting lesson or simply made a positive difference in someone else's life. Take the time to write these down on a piece of paper. Your personal stories should be ones that made you feel proud and that were ethically and morally sound (see examples Appendix page 113).

Feel free to include those experiences you are most excited about. Most people's dreams are lost early in life, usually between the ages thirteen and eighteen. *Give your dreams another chance!*

From your stories, you'll be able to see some very clear patterns of happiness and success, as well as a central theme that runs through each story. Now make a list of your obvious *strengths* revealed in those stories. Make a few notes about the areas you should avoid in the future. This does not mean these areas are weaknesses; in fact, quite often, the opposite is true. You may be a great accountant, for example, you do it very well, you make a lot of money at it, but you have always dreamed about being in entertainment. Then blend the two. Apply the skills you have learned in accounting to a career you are passionate about (Appendix pages 114 and 117).

Write down answers to the following questions. What are your:

Life strengths?
Areas to avoid?

Exercise 2: Your *Items* and *Successes*

Take a look through that old box stored in the garage, under your bed, in the attic, closet or basement; wherever you put the recognitions of success in things you love to do. This is a treasure trove of old memories that you'll want to include as *Items* and *Successes* in this exercise. Review your stories in Exercise 1. Later, you'll use these lists for your ideal, second, and third career option résumé *Items* and *Successes*.

Items

Most résumés are filled with items. *Items* state dry, dead facts. *Items* include the fact that you have a college degree, worked, have a certain amount of experience, were on the swim team in high school or helped raise money for a charity.

The benefits of an *Advantage-Driven Résumé* come from listing your *Items*. *Items* are facts that stand on their own. Write each one down, *even if you're sure you won't use it on a résumé.* Your previous life experiences, and how you feel about them, reveal what will and will not make you happy.

Examples of Bill Karlson's *Items*. Some are matched to Bill's career titles on page 118:

2,3	Repeat, long term coatings sales accounts: international refining, marine, pulp and paper, chemical and engineering firms
1,2,3	Planned and conducted high level coatings education seminars for Fortune 500 firms
1,2,3	Bachelor of Science degree, Marketing major
2,3	Certified through classes by National Association of Corrosion Engineers (NACE)
2,3	Can estimate industrial plant square footage
1,2,3	Has strong written and verbal skills
1,2	Married, and father of a terrific daughter!
2	East Brentwood Presbyterian (Chartered)
1	Certified Personnel Consultant
2	Certified snow ski instructor
2	National Ski Patrol (Inactive)
2	Spent several years in the Boy Scouts
1,2,3	Volunteer for United Way, Lions Club
1,2,3	Find reading materials of all kinds relaxing
3	Designed, installed and maintained sophisticated computer database and network
2,3	Helped design a web site on the Internet
2	Board of Directors – United Cerebral Palsy
1,2	Published writer and recorded public speaker
1,2	Joined Phi Kappa Tau fraternity in college
1,2	Army Rangers (ROTC college program)
1	Job fair speaker, CNBC New York, sponsor

Successes

Successes are previous accomplishments or goals achieved in your employment, sports, school, family, personal life, or on community or non-profit projects. Successes expand on *Items* where you made a significant difference or achieved measurable results. You might have had terrific grades in school while you worked a full time job and shared parenting with your spouse, been a star on the swim team, or raised the most money for your favorite charity. *Successes* are typically what you have accomplished with your *Items*. If you make a list of all your *Successes* you will have a better idea of the areas of your life that need to be restored for you to be totally fulfilled in your new career or job. Write your *Successes* in as few words as possible.

Examples of Karlson's *Successes* matched to career titles 1, 2, or 3 on page 119:

1	Substantially reduced costs through copyrighted human resources job matching system
1	Authored successful *GET TOP $$$ IN A JOB YOU LOVE!* series
2,3	Increased sales and profits on a multimillion dollar high performance protective coatings business, exceeding set sales goals
2	Managed General Motors and Ford accounts while introducing new high performance coatings
2,3	Directed engineering staff to profitable multimillion dollar, high performance coatings maintenance contracts
2,3	Responsible for contract negotiation with thousands of dollars in savings

1,2,3 Successfully maintained long-term sales relationships

2,3 Profitably sold high performance coatings in the western U.S. and Far East basin

1,2,3 Won the DuPont National Hard Hat Award two years running for outstanding performance as a field engineer

1,2 Elected to Patrol Leader, Troop Leader, Order of the Arrow, then Assistant Scoutmaster in Boy Scouts of America

1,2 Received congratulatory letter from United States President Lyndon Johnson for being member of first Boy Scout Troop to hike the C&O canal (180 miles) in nine days

1,2 Division Director, United Way of America, made successful video of fourteen agencies in one day

1,2 Achieved Million Dollar Circle status in recruiting candidate salary income

1 Passed national executive recruiting exam to become Certified Personnel Consultant; received congratulatory letter from the state governor

Now it is your turn to list all of the *Successes* in your life that made you feel good. (Appendix page 119.)

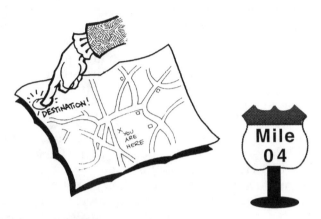

Where does your map lead?

Goal setting is the most powerful <u>Mile</u> of this career book. <u>Mile 04</u> prioritizes and sets an achievement date for your life goals.

A few years ago a laid-off sales professional came for help in getting another job after being fired. His own efforts had been dismal failures, even though he had been through several interviews. He couldn't figure out why he had not been hired by at least one of the companies he had seen. When I began to learn more about his job performance, I was as surprised as he. His work history was outstanding. He had continually increased sales and won several awards for excellence up until the previous few years. When we took the time to prioritize his goals, several facts came out that he had never taken the time to examine. His previous job had been great until he got married and had a son. Then the long grind of out of town travel, missed birthdays and two week absences began to wear on his marriage and happiness. Although he hadn't realized it, his goals had substantially changed and it had become impossible to "have it all." Something had to give. His performance on the job fell and he was let go because of his attitude. And what did I find him doing? He was sending résumés out to companies all over the country. When we completed his goals and put them in the order of real importance to him, family came out on top. No wonder his performance had fallen off. He was deliberately sabotaging his success to allow him more time at home. Yet even after being fired he was still sending résumés out for jobs that would force him to travel extensively and repeat the same process once again. He allowed a short term goal of financial security to override his long term goal of family values. After taking careful stock of his *Items* and *Successes,* we were able to get him on the path of a career with local opportunity and long term happiness.

Why take the time to prioritize and detail plans to achieve your goals? Because understanding the relationship between your various goals reveals what it will take to define your ideal career and make you happy. Only then will you be able to avoid the possibility of Life By Accident experiences.

You have two choices when putting your goals in order of importance. First, you can prioritize them by how you see things now. You might think you put family first, but over the previous few years, your job has caused *you* to miss many important family events. Your actions may prove that your career is more important and you accepted the trade-offs.

Or, you could prioritize your goals as you would like your life to be, changing jobs so that you are home more often. For example, is money really your top priority or do you simply have a short-term need for cash? Either way, total honesty with your package of skills, talents and temperament provides you with an exceptionally powerful tool to get you to your destination.

Read through the following goal options and order them in importance. Areas of your life that are not a high priority should be identified so that you can focus on areas of critical importance. It is also a way to reduce guilt. If being physically fit is not important, you can choose not to feel guilty the next time someone mentions your weight, or, move this goal up in your priority. The choice is yours.

Priority #	Goal
(#__)	**Career**
(#__)	**Community**
(#__)	**Family**
(#__)	**Financial**
(#__)	**Mental**
(#__)	**Physical**
(#__)	**Social**
(#__)	**Spiritual**

After prioritizing your goals, ask yourself and write down your answers *for each goal* to the following questions:

A. My short-range goal for the next six months and for the next five years?
B. *Expected obstacles* to achieving this goal?
C. *What* do I need to know to achieve this goal?
D. *Who* do I need to know and work with to accomplish this goal?

E. What is my list of *specific activities* with achievement dates for this goal?
   For example: By January 1, I will accomplish?
F. What's in it for me? How will I benefit from achieving this important goal?

(#__) Career Goal Option. You have an opportunity to explore three career options. Consider each option and the impact your life goals will have on your career.

Career Destination #1 (my ideal career choice). This is my long term dream, an industry or a job title which ignites an inexhaustible passion in me. **If I'd won the $100 million lottery and decided to continue working, this is what I would do.**
   There are several factors to consider when planning your career. How important is job satisfaction to your happiness? Does your job satisfaction depend on your ability to significantly contribute to your employment? Does it matter how your performance is measured? Does it matter who measures your contribution and performance? Does it matter if you can get promoted into another job or not? *Take time to think about the career you really want.* Write the directions needed to reach your *ideal* career destination by answering questions (A through F). Then complete your second and third career options.

A. My short-range goal for the next six months and for the next five years?
B. *Expected obstacles* to achieving this goal?
C. *What* do I need to know to achieve this goal?
D. *Who* do I need to know and work with to accomplish this goal?

E. What is my list of specific activities with achievement dates for this goal?
For example: By January 1, I will accomplish?
F. What's in it for me? How will I benefit from achieving this important goal?

Career Destination #2 (my second career choice). This is my second career path where I am willing to *compromise* when one of my other goals takes priority.

There are several factors to consider when planning your career. How important is job satisfaction to your happiness? In your second choice of a job, is job satisfaction dependent on your ability to significantly contribute to the work? Does it matter how your performance is measured? Does it matter who measures your contribution or performance? Does it matter if you can get promoted into another job or not? Take time to think about the career you really want. Ask yourself the following questions:

A. My short-range goal for the next six months and for the next five years?
B. *Expected obstacles* to achieving this goal?
C. *What* do I need to know to achieve this goal?
D. *Who* do I need to know and work with to accomplish this goal?
E. What is my list of specific activities with achievement dates for this goal?
For example: By January 1, I will accomplish?
F. What's in it for me? How will I benefit from achieving this important goal?

Career Destination #3 (my third career choice). This choice is minimally acceptable yet matches my prioritized goals. In other words, it gets the bills paid so that I can spend time doing something I actually enjoy. This may have been where you've spent a majority of your work life so far. Complete your third career option by answering the following:

A. My short-range goal for the next six months and for the next five years?
B. *Expected obstacles* to achieving this goal?
C. *What* do I need to know to achieve this goal?
D. *Who* do I need to know and work with to accomplish this goal?
E. What is my list of specific activities with achievement dates for this goal?
   For example: By January 1, I will accomplish?
F. What's in it for me? How will I benefit from achieving this important goal?

(#__) Community Goal Option. Success can be defined as being part of something bigger than yourself. Our love and concern for those outside our immediate family can be a great motivation. Many people participate in volunteer or charitable activities by themselves or with others. What can you contribute to your community, neighborhood, city, county, state, nation or the world?

A. My short-range goal for the next six months and for the next five years?
B. *Expected obstacles* to achieving this goal?
C. *What* do I need to know to achieve this goal?
D. *Who* do I need to know and work with to accomplish this goal?

E. What is my list of specific activities with achievement dates for this goal?
For example: By January 1, I will accomplish?
F. What's in it for me? How will I benefit from achieving this important goal?

(#__) **Family Goal Option.** What does your family mean to you? Do you treat your family with respect and courtesy all the time? Would they say you are a good listener? Does your family see you as a good role model? Are you tolerant and forgiving of others? How can you improve your marriage or personal relationships?

A. My short-range goal for the next six months and for the next five years?
B. *Expected obstacles* to achieving this goal?
C. *What* do I need to know to achieve this goal?
D. *Who* do I need to know and work with to accomplish this goal?
E. What is my list of specific activities with achievement dates for this goal?
For example: By January 1, I will accomplish?
F. What's in it for me? How will I benefit from achieving this important goal?

(#__) **Financial Goal Option.** What are your financial goals? Would you like to be debt free? What possessions are important to you? Which of those are important to your happiness? Some examples might include the purchase of a house, a new car, golf clubs or clothes. Do you have a savings plan for emergencies and retirement? Have you planned to meet your family's current and future obligations?

A. My short-range goal for the next six months and for the next five years?
B. *Expected obstacles* to achieving this goal?
C. *What* do I need to know to achieve this goal?
D. *Who* do I need to know and work with to accomplish this goal?
E. What is my list of specific activities with achievement dates for this goal?
   For example: By January 1, I will accomplish?
F. What's in it for me? How will I benefit from achieving this important goal?

(#__) **Mental Goal Option.** How important is it to keep your mind sharp? What are your plans for continuing education? What are you doing to stimulate your imagination? What materials do you read to further your career or personal interests?

A. My short-range goal for the next six months and for the next five years?
B. *Expected obstacles* to achieving this goal?
C. *What* do I need to know to achieve this goal?
D. *Who* do I need to know and work with to accomplish this goal?
E. What is my list of specific activities with achievement dates for this goal?
   For example: By January 1, I will accomplish?
F. What's in it for me? How will I benefit from achieving this important goal?

(#__) **Physical Goal Option.** Are you happy with your physical appearance? Do you have a healthy diet? Would you like to change your diet or exercise more? Have you planned for long-term, regular physical, medical and dental check-ups?

A. My short-range goal for the next six months and for the next five years?
B. *Expected obstacles* to achieving this goal?
C. *What* do I need to know to achieve this goal?
D. *Who* do I need to know and work with to accomplish this goal?
E. What is my list of specific activities with achievement dates for this goal?
   For example: By January 1, I will accomplish?
F. What's in it for me? How will I benefit from achieving this important goal?

(#__) **Social Goal Option.** Are you happy with your social life? Would you like to have more friends? What are you doing to maintain and enrich your relationships? Do you regularly contact the people who are important to your well-being? Can you develop your sense of humor?

A. My short-range goal for the next six months and for the next five years?
B. *Expected obstacles* to achieving this goal?
C. *What* do I need to know to achieve this goal?
D. *Who* do I need to know and work with to accomplish this goal?
E. What is my list of specific activities with achievement dates for this goal?
   For example: By January 1, I will accomplish?
F. What's in it for me? How will I benefit from achieving this important goal?

(#__) **Spiritual Goal Option.** Do you want a personal relationship with your choice of a Higher Power? If so, are you enriching your knowledge of spiritual texts? What are you doing to improve your serenity? Do you pray and meditate often?

A. My short-range goal for the next six months and for the next five years?
B. *Expected obstacles* to achieving this goal?
C. *What* do I need to know to achieve this goal?
D. *Who* do I need to know and work with to accomplish this goal?
E. What is my list of specific activities with achievement dates for this goal?
For example: By January 1, I will accomplish?
F. What's in it for me? How will I benefit from achieving this important goal?

Summarize what you have learned about your priorities and the effect they could have on your success, the choice of a career and your next job.

REST STOP

Throughout your career journey, it's important to take brief periods to review what you've accomplished so far. The real power of the *GET TOP $$$ IN A JOB YOU LOVE!*SM program comes from building your career one <u>Mile</u> at a time.

By considering each <u>Mile</u> thoroughly, you gain enthusiasm by focusing your energy in one direction. If you get stuck at a particular spot, it may help to go on to the next <u>Mile</u>. However, we strongly recommend working through <u>Miles 03</u> - <u>06</u> before you read the informational interviewing suggestions at the end of <u>Mile 06</u>.

If you have made notes to support your goals, check to see if the time lines you have set are realistic.

√ Know more about who you are in <u>Mile 02</u>
√ Build on the foundation of what you have to offer in <u>Mile 03</u>
√ Prioritize and list goal plans in <u>Mile 04</u>

Taking this reflective, <u>Mile</u>-by-<u>Mile</u> approach will help to ensure that you avoid future Life By Accident side trips.

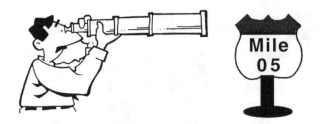

Identify your perfect job!

Welcome to <u>Mile 05</u>, where you get a close look at your ideal career and your next job. This time you get the chance to choose a job you'll be passionate about!

You now have a good feel for which work environment allows you to be most productive. You've looked beyond your current situation and it's time to define your first exciting career. A career that will make you happy and harmonize with what you have done.

Refining your career direction is time consuming, but definitely rewarding.

Information you wrote in your notebook in <u>Miles 02</u>, <u>03</u>, and <u>04</u> should be reviewed as you describe *your* first career choice. Go back now and take a look.

Define the ideal job that allows you to meet your prioritized goals by considering the following categories.

Consider your *ideal* career destination

Right now, it is worthwhile to take your pad and write answers to the following questions:

#1 Career *destination* (What you'd do if you won the lottery? It's okay, you'll be able to get realistic in the next <u>Mile</u>. See page 32.)

#1 Career job *title:* (If you are uncertain, you may want to wait until you have completed more research before you specify a career job title.)

Describe what you want in your first career choice:

Industry
Ideal career work duties and responsibilities
Location: 1st, 2nd, and 3rd choices
Base salary: $? Bonuses? Perks?
Work environment: (Review your five questions in <u>Mile 02</u> on page 20.)
Types of people to work around
Future growth and promotion likelihood
Travel: No ___ Yes ___ % time on the road___

Completing *all* your answers solidifies where you are going and how you intend to get there.

Other exciting career destinations!

At <u>Mile 06</u>, we offer you the opportunity to investigate other horizons. However, in <u>Mile 05</u> if you have a long-term dream, or found an industry or job title which sparked an inexhaustible passion, *go for it!* Delay investigating other careers until after you've reached a conclusion on your first choice.

On your career trip, you will recognize that other goals could affect your destination. Review <u>Mile 04</u> and make sure you're keeping true to yourself. For example, you've been in management and have had to travel frequently. Now you're forced to look for a new job. You were never happy on the road and now you have elderly parents in ill health. Your family is a higher priority than your career. Interviewing for another management job may be inappropriate, however, if it involves extensive or overnight travel. It could be another Life By Accident experience leading to yet another job search later.

Other goals may cause you to stay in a particular geographic location. Limiting your location usually means adding other career and job options. In the Appendix (page 122), you'll see that Bill Karlson has chosen a *second* career option in industrial sales, and a *third* as a corrosion coatings specialist, based on previous job experiences.

Look at your career goals again and describe *two other* exciting career destinations.

My second career choice!

#2 Career destination (This is my second career path where I am willing to *compromise* when my other goals take priority. See page 33.)

#2 Career *job title:* (If you are uncertain, you may want to wait until you have completed more research before you specify a career job title.)

Describe what you want in your second career option:

Industry
Preferred career work duties and responsibilities
Location: 1st, 2nd, and 3rd choices
Base salary: $? Bonuses? Perks?
Work environment: (Review your five questions in Mile 02 on page 20.)
Types of people to work around
Future growth and promotion likelihood
Travel: No ____ Yes ____ % time on the road____

Writing these down will give you clarity on where you are going and how you intend to get there.

My third career option!

#3 Career *destination* (This choice is minimally acceptable yet matches my prioritized goal, see page 34.)

#3 Career job title: (If you are uncertain, you may want to wait until you have completed more research before you specify a career job title.)

Describe what you want in your third option:

Industry
Preferred career work duties and responsibilities
Location: 1st, 2nd, and 3rd choices
Base salary: $? Bonuses? Perks?
Work environment: (Review your five questions in <u>Mile 02</u> on page 20.)
Types of people to work around
Future growth and promotion likelihood
Travel: No ___ Yes ___ % time on the road___

     Your third choice typically is not what you really want, but is acceptable as long as you are able to do what you would like off the job.
     Now that you have a basic idea of up to three different career paths, you'll head to your local library and the Internet to investigate attractive industries after completing <u>Mile 07</u>. Find definitions of specific titles for the alternative career paths you've chosen. For example, your ideal career title of *Data Processing Specialist* might have various job descriptions in different industries. A *Management Information Systems Specialist* in a manufacturing plant, or a *Medical Information Input Specialist* at a hospital, may require the same set of skills.

When you understand what each industry calls their positions you will have more opportunities to pursue.

Is this research <u>Mile</u> really necessary? How often do job descriptions perfectly match what people do? The fact is that job descriptions rarely match the work being done. To learn more about careers, locate these books in your library:

Occupational Outlook Handbook
Dictionary of Occupational Titles
Encyclopedia of Careers and Vocational Guidance
Professional Careers Source Book
101 Careers: Guide to Fastest Growing Careers
Career America - Federal Jobs
Adams Job Bank
or surf the Internet for other prime information. (See page 53.)

You may be one of the lucky few who has landed a totally fulfilling job. Your job matches your goals, keeps you interested and you're delighted to come to work each day. Many workers, however, are unsatisfied with their current job. Examine your situation and your chances for the future. Job security no longer exists and you soon may find yourself looking for another job – *just like the one you have.*

Every <u>Mile</u> of this program applies to you. Carefully examine each <u>Mile</u>, knowing that matching your goals to your career direction will come easier as you gather more information.

Your ideal job may be very close to what you are doing now, or have done recently. It may only be missing a few key elements that would enhance your life. *It is possible to find meaning in any job.* Here is an example from the automotive industry.

Carl had worked for a major automotive manufacturer for over thirty years. All of that time, he installed rear brake drums on pick-up trucks. The vehicles came down the line every sixty seconds and Carl had to make the same repetitive, boring motions. However, there was something different about the way Carl did his job. Unlike some of his younger co-workers, Carl avoided any diversion from the task at hand. No headsets with thumping music for him. On a break one day, someone asked Carl how he was able to stay so focused in such a boring job. He said he wasn't always so interested. Then one day, his son told him he was going to buy a pick-up made at Carl's plant. That day, Carl's entire view changed. "I never knew which truck was going to be hauling my grandbabies around; so ever since, I've made sure that every set of brake drums I put on is done *right!*" What can *you* find to make your job more meaningful?

Informational Interviews

Here are some suggestions about how to telephone people who are active in your chosen industry; people who work in jobs you are interested in.

Check your public library for directories of companies, organizations and institutions in your area. Identify those you think may have your occupational titles and also ask your friends and acquaintances which organizations may have these titles. Get names and telephone numbers of people you might want to interview informally.

Here is a suggested script to use when conducting *informational* interviews.

Hello, my name is _____. I am investigating a new career:___. (Career job title for this career destination.)

I need less than fifteen minutes of your time. Do you have a moment now?

Yes? Great!

Or, when would be a convenient time to call you back?___. I'll call back at ___.

Write down the name and title and make sure you call back on time.

I'd like to ask you a few questions about your career field (add *your* questions):

1. What do you love about your work?
2. How did you get into this field?
3. If you were getting into this field today, what would you do differently?
4. What are three key, job-specific performance elements required for this career field? (What must you be able to do professionally to get the job done?) (Appendix page 121.)
5. What skills do you most enjoy using?
6. What is the downside of this career?
7. What areas of growth, change, or new opportunities do you see?

Other questions could include those five questions (which you created in <u>Mile 02</u>) that you must have answers to before you can say "Yes" to a great job offer.

Ask: *"Could you suggest the names of two or three other people I could call to learn more about this career field?"* (Ask for telephone numbers. Ask if you can mention that you have had this conversation. Do *not* ask if you may use their name when introducing yourself to the people whose names you have been given.)

Your perfect employer research!

Let's find out which companies or organizations you'd like to pursue. What company would you really love to work for next? Using the proven concepts of *GET TOP $$$ IN A JOB YOU LOVE!* you will never again have to wait for someone else to take the initiative on your behalf.

A person with a strong background in commercial lending in the banking industry came to me after having been fired. He was devastated by the way it had been handled. He had been told at 9:05 in the morning and escorted out the door by two security guards at 9:15. Although he understood this was standard procedure it had never happened to *him*. He was uncertain about where he might even look for another job, having been with this same company over fifteen years. We took out a local list of top banks in the area, found over twenty, and he was well on his way through the list by mid-afternoon. He found two job openings and his confidence was restored in his ability to become reemployed quickly.

Ask your local *reference* librarian about using national standard industrial classification (S.I.C.) codes to locate companies in your industry. An exceptional information resource is the Internet (see page 53). Companies are becoming more active on the Internet through advertising, employer profiles, investors' reports, etc. Ask school libraries, colleges and universities if free access is available. If you have access to the Internet, search for companies, organizations and institutions in the industries you selected in Miles 05-06.

Now head for a library and find employers who do what you love.

Employer Matches to Career Destinations

My three career job titles (taken from pages 41, 43 and 44):

1.
2.
3.

Common Reference Sources

U.S. *Industrial Outlook*
Industry surveys
Industry reports
College placement offices/Alumni groups
Chambers of Commerce
Telephone company: your *ideal city* local Yellow
  Pages

Circulation Resources

America's Top 300 Jobs
Book Series, such as: *Opportunities In: Accounting/*
  Aerospace/ Culinary/ Electrical Trades/
  Health/ Medical/ Information Systems/ Law,

Finding Job Openings Reference Sources

Job Hunters Source Book
Where the Jobs Are: 1200 Journals Listing Career
  Opportunities
Dun's Career Guide
Peterson's Guide to Engineering/ Science/ Computer/
  Business/ Management Jobs
Business and Finance Career Directory

Executive Search/Professional Recruiters

National Association of Personnel Services
The Directory of Executive Recruiters (sometimes
  called the "red book")

National Periodicals

National Ad Search
National Business Employment Weekly
Federal Jobs Digest

General Employer Information

For Information on Public Companies:

Moody's Manuals
Standard & Poors Corporate Records, etc.

For Information on Public or Private Companies:

Dun & Bradstreet Million Dollar Directory
Directory of Advertisers
Dun's Business Rankings
Corporate Technology Directory
National Job Bank
(Interview customers or vendors of the companies to
    learn more.)

Information on Nonprofit Organizations

Nonprofit Corporations, Organizations and
    Associations

Local Periodicals
(Nashville, Tennessee, used as an example).

"Infotrac"
Business Nashville
InReview
Nashville Banner
Nashville Business Journal

The Nashville Woman
The Tennessean

The Internet

The Internet is extremely fluid. Sites you see today may not exist tomorrow and new career research locations appear every day. Use Internet search engines like:

Alta Vista: http://www.altavista.digital.com/
Lycos: http://www.lycos.com/
WebCrawler: http://www.webcrawler.com/
Yahoo: http://www.yahoo.com/

to find career sites like:

America's Job Bank offers a comprehensive database of jobs nationwide, which you can search by job title.

http://www.ajb.dni.us/

World Wide Web. The name says it all.

Career Action Center is a non-profit organization located in the San Francisco Bay Area. The Center is known nationally for advancing career self-reliance through programs and services which help individuals manage their work life in today's rapidly changing environment. Their web site includes information about the Center's resources and membership program, including weekly updates on programs, events, career management issues and links to other career management resources.

http://www.careeraction.org/

Career Magazine: a jump station to career-related resources. Resources are themselves meta-indexes, diverse and information-rich.

http://www.careermag.com/

Career Builder: find jobs from 70+ sites.

http://www.careerbuilder.com/

Career Resource: has information on employers, reference material, job databases and posts résumés for employers to search and browse. Some sites accept résumés in ASCII format.

http://www.careerresource.net/

Career Search Services on the Internet. The University of St. Cloud offers multiple listings of career openings, education jobs and on-line career search support. "Click" on University Resources.

http://condor.stcloud.msus.edu/

Career Strategies, Inc. offers bilingual career aptitude testing, career design seminars, job search counseling, résumé preparation and career counseling.

http://www.csinc.co.jp/eindex.html

Extreme Resume Drop is a proactive résumé site on the web that enables job hunters to send résumés directly to recruiters' e-mail boxes.

http://www.mainquad.com/resumedrop.html

FedWorld: opportunities with the federal government.

http://www.fedworld.gov/
http://www.state.edu/other/other.html

Helpwanted.Com: companies pay to put their job openings on this database.

http://helpwanted.com/

Hoover's Online: Company information doesn't have to be boring! Enjoy lively company profiles plus free access to 10,000 records on public and private companies. Get the latest stock quotes, quarterly earnings, SEC filings and more.

http://www.hoovers .com/

JobBank USA specializes in providing employment networking and information services to job candidates, employers and recruitment firms.

http://www.jobbankusa.com/

Job Hunt: On-Line Job Meta-List

http://www.job-hunt.org

Jobtrak: the big site to visit for job listings.

http://www.jobtrak.com

JobWeb: career planning and employment information, job search articles and tips; job listings and company information for college students, recent graduates and alumni. Sponsored by the National Association of Colleges and Employers.

http://www.jobweb.org

Mark Kantrowitz's "Financial Aid Homepage." This is an extremely useful site, catering to future, recent and "not so long ago" graduates.

http://www.finaid.org

Montana State University Career Services is primarily devoted to assisting all students in defining their career direction, major selection, internship location and job search assistance. Services are also available to alumni of MSU.

http://www.montana.edu/wwwcp/

The Recruiter OnLine Network: search firms and recruiters listings.

http://www .ipa.com/

Washington Jobs

http://www.washingtonpost.com/wl/home.shtml

The Catapult: a very comprehensive and well-organized index of all sorts of job listings and career guides.

http://www.jobweb.org/catapult/catapult.htm

The Internet's Online Career Center, montser.com, is one of the most comprehensive and frequently used on-line job search resources. It contains a large database of jobs searchable by type, locations, etc. You can also submit your resume to this service for employer and professional recruiter access.

http://www.occ.corn/

The Riley Guide: Employment Opportunities and Job Resources on the Internet is one of the most comprehensive and well organized list of Internet job resources.

http://www.dbm.com/jobguide

The ZONE is a plethora of WWW "links".

http://worldentre.com/mlmlnks.htm

VIRTUOCITY by VXR Corporation. Pronounced like "virtuosity," this electronic community is a virtual city in cyberspace of businesses and individuals engaged in commerce and other activities on the Internet.

http://www.virtuosity.com/

WinWay Corporation. Tired or bored with your job hunt? Need to take a break? Surf bored? Looking for other cool web sites? You've come to the right place.

http://www.winway.com/

Worklife. Australia's largest established support service to individuals who want to resolve career and work life issues providing career and life management services.

http://www.worklife.au/

Use the Employer Research Form on the following page to collect the information you have gathered on companies and the projects, new developments, or initiatives in which you are interested. With information from your library, the Internet and personal contacts (from page 46), you are now in a position to contact people. Call organizations to learn more about projects, new developments or initiatives. It is important to ask the same questions of different people in an organization because they will all have different perspectives.

We suggest you use, or adapt, the scripts on the following pages to interview people in sales, customer service, public affairs or elsewhere. This new information will fuel your career journey on <u>Mile 09</u>.

The purpose of this research is to learn more about the specific activity in a company that interests you. It will also give you an idea of the specific job performance elements of that activity.

You will use this information in <u>Mile 08</u> to create a résumé that uses the employer's job-specific performance elements to structure the basic format. These performance elements become statements of your *Advantages*. Your *Successes* and *Items* from <u>Mile 03</u> will be used to verify that you are able to meet the needs of your future employer.

Career path employer research information

Gather this information from employer contacts. Investigate current affairs, projects, new developments or initiatives by interviewing employer contacts in sales, customer service, public affairs, or elsewhere, including visiting their Web site.

(Some of this information may not be available.)

Career title
Industry
Employer
Years in Business
Address (at location you'd like to work/main headquarters)
Annual reports, industry contacts or customers
Number of local employees at your choice of location
With entire employer
Employer total company sales

Sales by this location
Profits this year
Profits last year
Profit growth % last year
Profit growth % previous five years
Sales growth % last year
Sales growth % previous five years
Product line/service you want to support

Suggested script to use when interviewing sales, customer service, or public affairs to discover what a company may be doing that matches your passion:

Hello, my name is _____.
I am a/an (job title for this career destination).
Have I caught you at a good time? Yes? Great! I need less than fifteen minutes. Or, when would be a more convenient time to call you back? I'll call back at?
Write down the name and title and call back on time!
I would like to ask you a few questions about what is happening at: (company name) and the (project, new development or initiative).
        Prior to your call, list questions you have about this employer and this project. Some questions about a new development or initiative might be:

What is its size, number of people and dollars?
What is the duration?
Does this company have all of the skills required to
        complete the project, new development or in-
        itiative within its existing work force?
What is the biggest obstacle to its completion?
Ask what are the three most important skills needed
        that would benefit this employer's cost of
        operation, profits, sales or help them fulfill
        their mission.

Some questions about the employer might be:

Which are your largest or most active product
    lines/services?
Which are most profitable?
Which are most likely to grow in the future?
Do employees have opportunities in all parts of the
    company or generally within one area?
Do employees get transferred often?

Ask for information on the person in charge of this
    project, new development or initiative as
    follows.
        Name:
        Title:
        Location:
        Telephone:

    Record information on special projects, activities, growth strategies, initiatives or new directions which you discover in your research.

    Now that you've had the exciting experience of working toward your goals, rather than just ambling along, you can begin to feel the power generated by being focused.

Having determined who you are and what you want, you have an idea of where you could work and if you will enjoy it.

Take some time to think about all the challenging decisions you've made so far.

√ In <u>Miles 05</u> and <u>06</u> you've considered the information necessary to arrive at your ideal career destination and other job options which meet your prioritized goals. Think about the choices you've made and reflect on how they blend together into a very powerful package to propel you into a great job.

√ In <u>Mile 07</u> you've determined the industries and employers that best meet your choice of career.

As you begin to successfully interview potential employers, you will be able to *avoid* Life By Accident jobs that will not meet your long term goals.

World's most powerful résumé!

Most people start their job search by *immediately* putting together what they believe to be an acceptable résumé. This résumé lists all the things they've done with strong emphasis on where they have had success in the past. It describes what they did for somebody else – which they hope will meet a future employer's needs.

Our experience has shown that résumés sent out "cold" (in response to an ad, or without previous introduction) get less than a 6% response rate. That means that 94 times out of 100 you will not hear *anything* from an ad you thought matched you perfectly. Talk about an esteem-robber! Here you are, really excited about taking this new career trip and someone has let the air out of your tires.

When giving public seminars, one of the approaches to proving my point about résumés is to request a sample from the audience. I'll ask the audience to decide which résumé they would prefer to read first. I also ask why. In the many years as a professional public speaker and job search seminar leader I have never had the audience choose the sample provided. They have always chosen my example over their peers. Why? A one page, concise, easy to read, filled with white space, *Advantage-Driven Résumé* simply overpowers any other style. More on this new style of résumé later in this Mile.

Many people think they'll find a new career or a good job by sending out résumés in response to newspaper want ads or directly to an employer's human resources department. But these options don't work well. We encourage you to send your résumé to want ads, while completing your work in this book. Go ahead and get it out of your system. If you actually *do* get a call, sound excited because you have beaten the odds! For a sample response to want ads, see Appendix page 137.

Why does sending a general résumé get such a poor response? You can't really know what a future employer needs. The résumé you're sending may read like an obituary in Sunday's newspaper, if it is just a chronological listing of what you did for previous employers. Most of these résumés get less than 10 seconds of review before they are *screened out.* To get the job, you need to attract the attention of the decision maker.

To give you an idea of what you will achieve by this exercise, look at the résumé you are using now. Give yourself *only 10 seconds* to read it (the time a real-life screener will invest). Judge its value, based on its appearance. Is it on one page, easy to read, with plenty of open space? Is your phone (or pager) number clearly visible? Can you list three reasons why a hiring authority would call you for an interview? Would *your* résumé be screened in or out?

Are you impressed with what you read? Does your résumé show how you can help a future employer reduce costs, increase profits or achieve the organization's objectives? If you're not impressed with what you see, let us give you a way to create the world's most powerful résumé.

Items, Successes and *Advantages*

Congratulations on getting this far on your new career journey. You've taken the time to investigate industries and job titles, you can sense a good fit for the future and feel confident that your goals are achievable. You've now passed the first seven <u>Miles</u> and should have all your goals prioritized, each supported by a thoroughly detailed plan.

The *Items, Successes* and *Advantages*ˢᴹ (*ISA*ˢᴹ) concept is new to many people and takes a little getting used to. Just remember that *Items* and *Successes* are things you have done previously. *Advantages* are benefits you can bring to your next employer.

You will use this <u>Mile</u> to plan your career résumé(s). There are descriptions and résumés using the *ISA* concept (Appendix page 123). As you work through this <u>Mile</u>, you may find that you feel differently about the career titles you have previously chosen. This is the time to go for what you really want. Feel free to make changes and get comfortable with your new career path options.

Begin thinking about what you want your future résumé to say about your advantages. Then write down three basic job-specific performance elements that are critical to success in each of your career options. Refer to the key performance elements you discovered in <u>Miles 05</u>-<u>07</u> while conducting informational interviews with people in these career fields.

Your ideal career title #1_____.

Three key job-specific performance elements you need for career destination #1_____.

Your career title #2_____.

Three key job-specific performance elements you need for career destination #2_____.

Your third career title_____.

Three key job-specific performance elements you need for career destination #3_____.

Think about your most recent job, or what you have done previously, that you can use to support your interest in a specific job. What are the three most important job skills you have that could be used as future *Advantages* for a new employer? These must relate to the key job-specific performance elements. Take a look at the *Items* and *Successes* you've created in <u>Mile 04</u>. Now, turn them into at least three generalized *Advantage* statements, *written in future tense* for each of your career destinations. What do your previous accomplishments reveal about what you can do for a future employer? *Don't expect the hiring authority to make the connection between what you accomplished for another employer and what you can do for them; especially if you're looking at a job in a different industry!*

It is important to remember that your *Advantages* are the reasons your future employer will want to hire you. See Bill's résumés in the Appendix pages 126, 129 and 132.

For example, for Bill's second career choice, there are three industrial sales *Advantages* that would cause a future employer to put the résumé in the "TO BE CALLED!" short stack:

1. Can show profitability gains through communication skills.
2. Will make an excellent first impression with top clients.
3. Can achieve profitability goals.

Other *Advantages* to hiring Bill from the sales résumé:

Can bring professionalism to business.
Can successfully maintain long term sales relationships.
Brings communication and interpersonal skills to challenging situations.
Through unique approaches, can increase sales to achieve substantial profitability gains.

Now it's time to use the *Items, Successes,* and *Advantages (ISA)* that you have developed. Each résumé will match your skills, talents and knowledge to the specific needs of the employer or industry you've researched in <u>Miles 05</u>-<u>07</u>. Examine what you have to offer a future employer. Think about the *Advantages* which will help reduce costs, increase sales or profits, or achieve the organization's mission and objectives.

List three *Advantages* for your ideal career destination. These are three things you will need to be able to do professionally to be successful in this job. Write them in *future tense.*

Now list other reasons for an employer to hire you, *written in future tense.*

List three *Advantages* each for your second and *third* career destinations. These are three things you would have to be able to do professionally to be successful in these jobs. Write them *in future tense.* Now list other reasons for an employer to hire you, *written in future tense.*

The purpose of this <u>Mile</u> has been to get you to take a fresh look at why an employer would want to hire you. It's usually irrelevant to an employer what *you* want when an interviewer is screening applicants. They're only concerned about what you can do for them. Can you solve the problem they are faced with today, or not?

Knowing the exact needs of an employer you'd like to work for puts you significantly ahead in the job race. Documenting how you can meet those needs gives you the world's most powerful résumé, as you'll discover in <u>Mile 09</u>.

When you have finished, you'll have an *Advantage-Driven Résumé* listing your *Advantages,* supported by your *Items* and *Successes* that will entice a hiring authority to place it in the "TO BE CALLED!" short stack.

Please note that we do not recommend a written career profile, career objective, personal information, graduation dates or employer locations on your résumé.

If you are a Vietnam veteran, put it down. The Vietnam Era Readjustment Assistance Act of 1974 (38 U.S.C. 4212) prohibits job discrimination and requires affirmative action for qualified veterans on any Federal or subcontracted Federal job.

Your commonly used name (Bill, not William L.) should appear in bold 18 point type (centered), followed by your address in 9 point typeface and pager number in 12 point bold typeface. (See the example on page 126.) Why a pager? This might seem like too much trouble or expense, especially if your finances are limited.

Consider the benefits of having a pager. Suppose Mary Lou and Barbara Anne both applied for their ideal career at Widget Maker, Inc. Ms. Hiring Authority is impressed by both résumés and calls each to schedule an interview, but is unable to reach either directly. Both job hunters are busy researching industries and calling references. They do not return home until late Friday night. Monday morning at 9:00 a.m. sharp, Barbara Anne quickly and professionally returns Ms. Authority's call. Her assistant, however, explains that Ms. Authority will be meeting with another candidate all morning and is unable to take the call. Mary Lou smiles to herself as she sits in Ms. Authority's waiting area and overhears the assistant's conversation.

Which person has the pager and was able to quickly contact the hiring authority? A pager can give you a twelve hour head start on your competition!

Now, a note on cover letters. The bad news first. Multi-paragraph, detailed covers letters are rarely read by employers. *These folk simply do not have the time to read what you want from them.* After all, how do you know what they need without the research we mentioned earlier in the book?

The good news is that brief, specific employer-targeted cover letters can help you land an interview. Your résumé should go directly to the hiring authority you've identified after a professional telephone presentation and the client acknowledges a need and their interest in you (Mile 09). We suggest a one paragraph introduction, stating you have already spoken to the person receiving your information (discussed in Mile 09). Thank them for their time; set a date and time you will call to confirm that they received your résumé (*make sure to call when you said you would*). If they are not available, leave a message confirming your call and try again later. Our approach stresses the *Advantage-Driven Résumé* nature of your search. Build a match between the employer's needs and your business *Advantages.*

Follow up now by completing the résumé format on the following pages, directly targeting the careers you have researched and chosen. Remember, your *Advantage-Driven Résumé* might change for each application, because you have discovered at least three different *Advantages* you've discovered for each particular job title.

See Bill's résumés in the Appendix, pages 126, 129 and 132.

Each Mile of this trip is building towards empowering you with a sense of excitement and hope.

Job specific (matching the title of the job you want)
Advantage-Driven Résumé information
for my career choice as a ____

Informal Name

(Centered 18 point bold)

Address:

_____

_____

_____

_____

(Centered 9 point plain text)

Message (____) _____
(Centered 10 point plain)

Pager (____) _____
(Centered 12 point bold)

Refer to your employer research work in <u>Mile 07</u> to match your *Items, Successes* and *Advantages* with your future employer's needs. *Advantages* and dates should be in 12 point bold typeface. Use your strengths, *Items* and *Successes* from pages 25, 26 and 28, which should be in twelve point regular face type. (Appendix pages 126, 129, and 132.)

Your résumé and Internet basics

A computer network is created when two or more computers are linked together electronically. Network users can access information in other computers and upload it to their own computer, print hardcopy and upload information to send to other computers. Over the last few years, thousands of computer networks have been linked together. This combined set of networks is called the "Internet."

The Internet is a very large community where information is shared freely between users and is also a rapidly expanding commercial marketplace.

The Internet was initiated by the U.S. Department of Defense to share information more effectively. Previously, they had shipped reels of computer tape and punched cards among the departments, universities and military contractors. The National Science Foundation is among those who have financially supported it. Other financial supporters include organizations and individuals who create databases and freely share them. Commercial enterprises are now becoming significant players on the Internet, supplying both free and fee-based services.

Employers are now listing their job openings on the Internet and you can readily access this information. At the same time, candidates list their résumés on the Internet. Employers and third-party recruiters daily search the Internet for résumés that meet their requirements.

Accessing the Internet, Résumés and Jobs

An introduction to *Employment Opportunities and Job Resources on the Internet* is available online without charge and is updated from time to time (http.//www.jobtrak.com/jobguide/). This guide was created by Margaret F. Riley, circulation and computer resources librarian at Worcester Polytechnic Institute's Gordon Library in Worcester, Massachusetts.

Subscribing to commercial online services via your home computer is one way to job search on the Internet. These services include America Online (800-227-6364), CompuServe (800-848-8199), Genie (800-638-9636), Prodigy (800-776-3449) and others. Other options include your local public library, colleges, universities, and career and job search assistance organizations such as state employment service offices.

We recommend putting résumés for each of your career paths on the Internet. Executive recruiters and employers browse this powerful resource daily for candidates.

Electronic résumés are different from paper résumés in many respects. Some, but not all, of the differences are:

- They must be prepared within the limits of ASCII format (plain text)
- Line length is limited to 65 characters
- Keywords, which label your skills, must be used to avoid being passed over
- Use regular (Roman) typeface (nothing in **bold** or *italic*).

A person reading your résumé will be able to view only 20 lines at a time; therefore, your *Advantage-Driven Résumé* (in plain 12 point text) lends itself to a powerful, hard-hitting approach, beautifully designed to market your skills on the Internet.

How to get your résumé on the Internet

As you learned in your Internet research, there are many different places to load your résumé. Most require nothing more than the ability to e-mail your text to a location. To date, loading your information is free and will be accessed by hundreds of potential employers.

Many local colleges and all major universities have Internet access and provide résumé loading services to students. Check it out! (See pages 53-60.) Other excellent resources are Fred E. Jandt's and Mary B. Nemnich's *Using the Internet and the World Wide Web in Your Job Search,* and Joyce Lain Kennedy's *HOOK UP, GET HIRED! – THE INTERNET Job Search Revolution.*

Congratulations! Having done the work (and when did you ever achieve something truly worthwhile without effort?), you're on the right path.

Your commitment and your focus on your career path are now exceptionally strong. Take a few minutes to look over everything you've considered so far.

√ <u>Mile 08</u> caused you to organize and plan the key elements necessary to successfully match your skills and interests with a new career path (or

job) through your *Items, Successes* and *Advantages.*
You took everything you've done so far and sum-
marized it into incredible *Advantage-Driven
Résumés.* These résumés will give you a much
greater chance of being placed in the "TO BE
CALLED!" short stack.

It's time to use one of the most powerful approaches ever developed to achieve the career of your
dreams; *Positive* networking in <u>Mile 09.</u>

Positive networking!

"Isolation is the dream killer, not your lousy attitude. Sort of like a horse raised in a basement, you know *something* just isn't right."　　　　*– Barbara Sher*

Regardless of education background, unique skills or your previous performance, quickly preparing a new résumé is not the best way to begin your job search. Many people then compound that damage by taking what they think is their next logical step; they begin calling their business friends and associates and explaining their situation.

Most people believe "networking" means *immediately* asking people if they know of any job openings. We call this negative networking. It's important not to isolate yourself, but this approach doesn't work very well. Why not?

How would you feel if an acquaintance called you at work? Their voice is a little shaky as they tell you they've lost their job. You can hear the pain and the fear in their voice. If this is a former business competitor asking about openings at your company, is there a *slight* chance that you might want to protect your own future?

When they asked for leads, how many were you prepared to provide? Do you want them talking to your boss? Would you give out telephone numbers of those you know and respect, or who respect you? You might become concerned about your own future. After all, if it could happen to them, it could also happen to you. Would you like to learn about *positive* networking that yields much better results?

Networking is a very powerful tool if you do it right. Doing it right means pulling together all of the effort you've made so far in this book. What's the single most important factor in a person's positive networking success? *Passion.* Passion for the next opportunity to excel in a job you really want to have. Try networking to find a job just like the one you used to have. You know, the one you used to hate until you lost it. You sound disinterested on the phone because you are less than enthusiastic about having an employer offer you another opportunity to be bored or stressed. By choosing an opportunity that matches your previous *Items* and *Successes*, meets your prioritzed goals, and fulfills a personal mission, your *passion* is inescapable and infectious.

Make sure you can offer your next employer ways to *improve their performance, reduce costs or increase their profits.* By far the best way to communicate this is to use your *Advantage* statements written in <u>Mile 08</u> for each specific career path.

Everything you've worked so hard to complete on this journey will be used to put you ahead of your competitors. Everyone has unique experiences, skills and talents. By using the *Items, Successes* and *Advantages* concept, your immediate value is instantly clear to a hiring authority.

You have completed your career path research, know exactly which companies fit your ideal job (or second and third, if necessary), and who is the decision maker for the job you want. Now it's time to prepare a script. This may sound unusual if you have never *positively* networked, been in sales or worked in telemarketing.

Landing the career of your dreams requires working at least forty hours a week. Part of this effort is understanding that it will take multiple calls using our professional, *positive* networking techniques to uncover your ideal job.

The script is built from your earlier efforts to determine the three most important *Advantage*s you have to offer a new employer and your preparation in writing your *Advantage-Driven Résumé*. You'll want to write a script that *compels* the decision maker to interview you.

Your scripts are an introduction for each of your career destinations. They include your three main *Advantages* and build on your research and your *ISA* preparation. When you call, a script breaks the hiring authority's concentration, it is courteous and quickly gets to the point. You'll have your complete *ISA* in front of you, as well as your specific research on the employer you're calling.

Consider using the following format. *Once you achieve a level of comfort in using these scripts, write them in your own style.*

The career I would like to pursue

(career destination's job title and location)

Doing your homework, knowing something about the employer and your career options (1, 2 or 3) is critical to using this script successfully. Review your work from <u>Mile 07</u> starting from page 61 before developing your script.

Be ready to ask your list of five questions, the ones that must be answered before accepting a new career assignment (<u>Mile 02</u> from page 20).

Remember that each career path will have a unique ISA, résumé, set of job duties and employer description.

Now it's time to develop your script for calling this employer's hiring authority. You will call the person who can say "Yes" to hiring you: the person in charge of the project, new development or initiative (see page 63). Be sure to have the hiring authority's name and correct title before calling.

Hiring authority name:
Title:

Practice your script with friends or family before making your call.

Use the following script **when calling the employer's hiring authority:**

Hello, my name is _____. *(Don't laugh; in the excitement of a great call, you may forget to introduce yourself.)*

I am passionate about (career job title for this career destination)
Have I caught you at a good time? Yes? Great! I'll need less than fifteen minutes of your time.
Or, when would be a convenient time to call back?
I'll call back at _____.

I am interested in getting involved in your (project, new development, or initiative, etc.). *I have a real passion for this type of employment.* (This information comes from your employer research in Mile 07.)

I would like to ask you five questions about what is happening at (employer name):
1._____?
2._____?
3._____?
4._____?
5._____?

My Advantages include: (Have your *Advantages* from Mile 08 written below and ready to discuss.)

1._____.
2._____.
3._____.

I think my abilities would greatly assist (employer name) (project, new development or initiative, etc.)
Would it be possible to schedule a time to discuss this option in greater detail?

Sometimes an employer will ask for your résumé. If practical, offer to deliver it in person. If you are asked to fax a copy, always follow up the fax by mailing a quality hard copy to the potential employer.

Write down:

Date _____
Time _____
Location _____.

If you have found an opening, or have a reason to call back, complete:

Notes about _____ (employer).
Person to contact (ask for spelling, correct title and work phone with extension):
Title:
Work Phone/Extension:
Hiring authority or other decision maker, if different:
Title:
Work Phone/Extension:

What the job requires; and your matching *Advantages:*

Three things I have to be able to do professionally to be successful in this job:

1._____.
2._____.
3._____.

My matching *Advantages:*

1._____.
2._____.
3._____.

I'd like to suggest one final networking technique that Dr. Bernard Haldane shared with me. He believes, as I do, that *everyone you meet can, in some way, help you achieve your dream.* The trick is to listen and be willing to risk in sharing what you want to do. He recommends asking everyone you meet to critique your information. Listen carefully to what they have to say. They may just have the key for you to start getting top dollars in a job you'll love.

Questions about *Positive* networking

Question 1: "How do I get past the secretary or assistant who is screening calls for the hiring authority?

Response: "I have abilities Ms. Manager of the project, new development or initiative may need. I need just a few minutes to tell her how I can help her."

Question 2: "How can I make these calls while still employed, if my present employer is incredibly well-networked?"

Response: "This is a tough problem. It depends on how unhappy you are in your present job. Understand you are taking a risk by putting your name out there."

What it will take!

If you're looking for a job, how do you know if you've had a good day?

How do you stay "positive" in your search?

One man was having a very difficult time staying on path while looking for his next job. He had completely shut down for two days before giving me a call. He spent the days in bed, periodically turning on the television as a distraction. You can imagine the challenge he had explaining how he had spent his day when the wife came home from her tedious job. We found that all of his work to this point was sound. All he needed was some incentive to get back on the phone and reawaken his passion. Setting up an hourly call number target did the trick.

He quickly became excited once again about his search and was back on the phone, with success, the next day.

This plan will help you achieve your ideal career or simply your next job. All you have to do is accumulate 50 markers-a-day, based on our marker system. This plan establishes a method of measuring your effort and performance.

Keep track of your achievements as professional recruiters do. This is a powerful way to avoid the possible loss of self-esteem and depression that often results from the routine rejections while looking for a new job. If you achieve 50 markers by lunch, reward yourself and enjoy the afternoon. The overall objective is 250 markers a week. If you have a light marker day (or two), you'll need to make up those markers to keep yourself on track.

We have some great news! All the effort you'll expend in reaching your new career goal counts. In getting to this Mile, give yourself a head start of 250 markers, or a full week of work. Your efforts, so far, dramatically shorten the time you'll need to reach your career destination.

What about your other activities, like responding to want ads, writing thank you letters, or checking-in with friends for moral support? These are meaningful activities, but don't count towards the measured activity required for achieving the career of your dreams.

There are numerous time management planners. We have found Stephen R. Covey's <u>Seven Habits Organizer</u> to be a highly-effective way of integrating your weekly goals. An electronic version works in conjunction with Microsoft Windows95 <u>Schedule Plus</u>. We also recommend <u>First Things First</u> by Stephen R. Covey, A. Roger Merrill and

Rebecca R. Merrill. Contact the Covey Leadership Center at 1-800-632-6839.

Accumulate *50 markers-a-day* for your next career destination

Activity	Description	Award
Calls made	Any call made directly related to getting yourself a job.	**01**
Networking	Getting leads to call; going directly to one of the employers researched; each person that gives you an informational interview.	**05**
Job Opening!	*Any* open job you find counts.	**10**
Phone interview	A phone interview with a hiring authority for an open job.	**05**
Interview	A face-to-face interview with the hiring authority.	**20**

Sending résumés to want ads, talking to friends about non-job issues, and other non-productive contacts do not get *any* marker awards. There is no point in rewarding activity that will not get you what you want.

REST STOP

You're getting close to the most exciting part of your career trip – *interviewing.*

    √ As you learned to *positive* network in <u>Mile 09</u>, your skills in discussing your career passion and *Advantages* for the future improved greatly.
    √ You've hit a few potholes in <u>Mile 10</u> and survived making the calls necessary to uncover the real opportunities you want to pursue.

    Before presenting yourself for any telephone or face-to-face interview, go back through all of the preceding <u>Miles</u> and mark key areas you want to reference. Highlight your notepad for any areas you'll want to reference later. If you're using a computer, set-up a new word processing document and duplicate any information you'd like to access quickly.
    Make a photocopy of the pages in your notebook that support what you want to do. With the interviewing preparation pages in <u>Mile 11</u>, *put together a package that you can quickly reference during telephone and face-to-face interviews.*

Going for top starting salary!

Mile 11 details some of the toughest roads you may travel enroute to your ideal job. We will show you how to ensure the top starting salary. Let's go!

What do you wear to your interview? We suggest you dress like a professional, *regardless* of where the interview is or who you're scheduled to meet. Freshly-pressed clothes, like bank executives wear, are appropriate. Colors in dark grays, dark blues, with polished shoes and matched accessories are a must. *You only get one chance to make that first impression.*

Here are some interviewing suggestions:

- Invest in a quality note pad and a pen-and-pencil set for taking notes.
- Leave your briefcase at home.
- Find out names and titles of the people who will be interviewing you.

- Bring business cards, which include your name, address, pager number and thank you notes and stamped envelopes.

Do not use your existing or former employer's business cards. This gives an unprofessional impression, particularly if you're still employed.

- Give each of your interviewers your business card and ask for theirs.
- Confirm that you have the correct name spelling and title.
- Write the *time* of your meeting on the back of their business card (I will explain later).
- Make notes of their main business concerns and your *Advantages*.
- Listen to what the interviewer has to say.
- Make a note about what you said, matching your *Advantages* to their needs.

Travel Suggestions

Make your own travel arrangements, where possible. Ask the employer representative if you can arrange you own flight schedules and put your travel expenses on their company's credit card. Make sure you know specific information about hotels, rental cars and directions to the employer's business before you leave for the interview. When you arrive in that city, drive to the employer's location at least once before your interview and ask the hotel about local traffic patterns.

- Do *not* check your luggage. Take a carry-on bag.
- Confirm your flight, hotel and rental car

reservations; get confirmation numbers.
• Note your confirmation numbers and ask
for your seat selections in advance.
• Have your airline tickets in hand the day be-
fore you travel, and check for accuracy.
• Keep all receipts.
• Easy on meals you charge to the employer.

Dinner Meetings

Hiring authorities will observe your social
skills and ability to make others feel comfortable at
the meal table. Choose small portions that can be ea-
ten neatly and quickly. You might also be judged on
how you handle alcohol. It's all right to order *one*
drink if the hiring authority does first, but nurse it
over the whole meal. Don't smoke unless invited to
do so, and then only if the other person smokes first.

Thank You Letters

Take several pre-addressed, stamped envelopes with you to the interview. Write a brief thank
you note to every person in the interviewing process
who could impact your hiring decision *(especially*
any administrative assistants). Thank them for their
time and then restate their issues and your *Advantages. Put these notes in the mail on the day of the interview.*
In the interview, the greatest challenges
you'll face will be deciding how to present your *Advantages*, discussing the issue of money, and discovering how you stand against the other candidates.
We'll show you how to negotiate the best salary and
benefits package in Point #3.

The following interviewing and negotiating points work. They will ensure you arrive at your career destination. We recommend this approach to prepare yourself for successful interviews. Practice the responses until they become natural. Use your own words, but stay with the basic principles of each approach.

Point #1

When the hiring authority asks, "So tell me about yourself," say: *"I have a number of important Advantages I feel I can bring to (employer's name). But rather than talk about things that may not match your needs, I'd appreciate if you would tell me a little more about the specifics of what you're looking for."*

Then, respond to the job requirements mentioned with your specific *Advantages* that match the employer's needs. Have the package of materials that you have developed from *GET TOP $$$ IN A JOB YOU <u>LOVE</u>!* ready to reference.

Point #2

At the appropriate time in the interview, ask the five questions you wrote down in <u>Mile 02</u> (from page 20). You must have answers to these questions before you can determine if you want the job *(do not ask compensation or benefits questions yet).*

Questions could include: what you need to know about a typical work day, important projects, job priorities, special knowledge that may be needed, travel requirements, the promotional path or overtime. (Avoid asking salary or benefits questions until you have an offer.)

Point #3

During one of my recruiting efforts a client company asked me to find a chemical engineer. At the time this was a very challenging request because these people were in very short supply. To make matters worse for me the salary this company was able to offer was on the low end of the scale. After extensively searching for several weeks without success, a recent chemical engineering graduate gave me a call and came by the office. Although she had no experience, my client was willing to see her. When asked how much money she felt was reasonable for the position, she said nineteen thousand dollars a year.

I told her that this was in the employers range, and asked her to follow some basic principles in the interview. One of these was never to accept an offer on the spot. Another was to call me immediately after the interview ended to debrief.

Within a few minutes of the interview ending she called me as asked. Unfortunately she was crying so hard that I could not make sense of what she was trying to tell me. I asked her to return home, which was close by, and call me back after she had calmed down.

In the meantime I received a concerned call from the client hiring authority. He stated that they were sincerely interested in my candidate and had extended an offer. Instead of responding she had burst into tears and quickly left his office. He said that he had gone over everything he had said and could find nothing wrong. He also offered to increase the salary offered by four thousand dollars if necessary.

I told him that I had received a call from the candidate but would have to call him back later.

Several hours later I heard from the candidate again. She told me she had been shopping for a car! I asked why she had left the office abruptly and had been crying during her first call. She told me that the offer had been thirty-eight thousand dollars a year, that she did not know what to say and had followed my advice not to accept on the spot! I explained that crying and leaving were not part of my training even if it worked so powerfully!

Understand that the hiring authority felt they may have offered too little while the candidate was overwhelmed by the amount! She officially accepted the first offer the next morning and has had a very fulfilling career at the plant site.

For top pay, I suggest following this powerful approach to the money question:

Hiring Authority: "I notice that you left the previous salary information blank on your application. What kind of money do you think you'd need to come to work for us?"

Candidate: "That's a terrific question; are you prepared to make me an offer?"

Hiring Authority: "Well, we have several candidates to see and we're getting a feel to see if you fall in our range financially."

Candidate: "May I ask you a few questions on that issue?"

Hiring Authority: "Please, go ahead."

Candidate: "Have I the qualifications for this job?"

Hiring Authority: "Yes." (If you don't have the qualifications, why are they talking with you?)

Candidate: "I feel the same way about my *Advantages.* I also think they closely match your needs. On a personal note, I would be very interested in learning what it is I have to offer that you think is special. What makes me stand out from other candidates?"

Hiring Authority responds with appropriate special talent. Even if you are the first candidate they have seen, you can make such an impression they will want to hire you.

Candidate: "*I'm glad to hear that you believe I am qualified and have a special talent for your job. I would like to make an unusual commitment to you now. I want this job and feel confident that we will work out the money issue. The reality is that it doesn't matter what I made or what I want. All that matters is what you feel is fair market value for my services. Based on the fact that you know I want the job, have the basic qualifications, and can bring special talents to your company, I feel I am worth the top salary offered. Let me know that number; I'll consider it carefully and call you at a convenient time tomorrow.*"

What happens if hiring authority says "We can't tell you that." Candidate responds with *"Would you let me know the range for the job?"*

How can you feel that you are getting the top starting salary?

By never accepting an offer on the spot. Once an offer is made, say you will give it careful consideration and call them back the next day. When returning the call to the hiring authority, say:

Candidate: *"Mr. Hiring authority, I want this job. Thank you for your offer yesterday. I have not changed my commitment to come to work for you. However, the offer was not exactly what I had expected to hear. Can you do any better?"*

The candidate then stops talking and listens to the hiring authority.

Alternate responses:

1. Hiring Authority: "No, we can't."

Candidate: *"OK, well, I am still happy to accept your offer, but I would like to ask for a salary review in six months, if my performance is strong enough to warrant it."*

2. Hiring Authority: "Yes, we can go to _____ or, we can offer _____."

Candidate: *"Thank you very much. On that basis, yes, I can accept your offer ..."*

Accept the offer at this point.

Even if the financial offer does not go up

substantially, you have the opportunity to ask for a salary review, based on your strong performance after six months. This ensures that you will receive the best possible salary in your first year of employment.

This approach ensures you're starting your new job with the best pay. One professional who used this approach achieved a 12.5% increase in salary, by asking the question and then being silent until the hiring authority responded with a better offer.

What happens if they don't say anything at all? Say nothing. Just wait for them to respond.

Negotiating an offer

Remember, *never* accept an offer immediately. There are other areas open to negotiation before you accept. However, an entry level position may be limited in extra perks and negotiating power. With careful questioning the day after an offer is extended you may be pleasantly surprised at the additional salary or benefits you can receive just by asking.

At higher salary or management levels, you are expected to negotiate beyond the basic package offered. In fact, *failure to ask for more than the minimum will leave your political savvy in doubt.* (If you are employed, do not resign your position until there is a signed offer from the hiring authority detailing the specifics of the total package. See the resignation letter on the Appendix page 133.)

The same is true if you are looking for a new job while unemployed. *Anything not written down prior to acceptance may disappear should your new employer have a change of management or economic downturn. Ask the employer to fax you their signed offer; you add issues important to you, then you sign and fax back your acceptance.*

After reviewing the following list, circle the areas which are important to you in your next job *before they make you an offer. This means that you have reviewed the employer's standard benefits* . For example, you know that they give two weeks vacation. You want three weeks, and make a note to include this in your formal acceptance. If it is applicable, you'll also want to know what the relocation package will be and whether the employer will pay for temporary housing.

Consider the following areas of negotiation *prior* to accepting an offer of employment

1. Base salary (minimum acceptable; "I expect to earn x" within one year). Ask if company policy allows for a review and increase in six months.

2. Bonus program *in writing!* (When given? How measured?)

3. Stock options (can tax considerations accrue to you?).

   a. Purchase price to be established by offer acceptance date. Can buy stock immediately after acceptance if possible and desired.

   b. Investment options. May make cash investment in the firm if desired at guaranteed rate of return.

   c. Ownership/control/voting options.

4. Vacation (When, how long, first time available, standard holidays)

5. Parachute options

   a. What constitutes non-performance? (Agreed to before signing)

   b. How much do you receive?

   c. When do you receive payment under your parachute? (cash)

6. Employer perks

   a. Employer car

   b. Access to corporate transportation (plane, cars, boats, etc.)

   c. Paid professional memberships

   d. Paid entertainment memberships (country club, golf, etc.)

7. Negotiation of non-compete agreement (if required) How long, restrictions, legal issues on client retention, etc.

8. Standard medical, dental, vision benefits

   a. Confirm all important medical areas (consider asking for exemption from pre-existing conditions).

   b. If dental is not offered and you have children, ask for a special policy to cover these expenses.

9. Relocation package (buy home, points, closing, fees, incidentals)

10. Other areas of negotiation and discussion

    a. Cafeteria style options

    b. Employee life and dependent life insurance

    c. Employer car; type, purchase on turnover

    d. Pension program (negotiate vesting date, if legally possible)

    e. Profit sharing

    f. Deferred compensation

    g. Eye and ear special coverage

    h. Savings program-401K, etc.

    i. Financial planning assistance

    j. Tuition refund

    k. Computer, dictating equipment, modem, paid home telephone

    l. Paid memberships, committee and professional participation

    m. Expense and entertainment accounts

n. Paid mileage on employer business

o. Paid health club membership; part of wellness program

p. Paid education expense allowance per year (time and money for seminars, books, tapes, software, etc.)

Point #4

Even if you are fully prepared for your interview, you will sometimes be thrown a curve-ball (an unexpected question not associated with anything you were prepared to discuss). For example, one of our clients was interviewing for the Executive Directorship of a local art gallery. In the middle of her interview, one of the interviewers asked her, "How would you explain 'blue' to the blind?" She was prepared for this type of question, but she saw no correlation between this curve question and what the administrative position required. Our suggestion for these curve-questions:

Hiring Authority: Asks a curve-question.

Candidate: This may be an opportunity to show your creative side or that you are prepared to accept tough challenges and stay engaged. Attempt to answer the question in order to show that you are nimble-minded or courageous enough to tackle it.

"All the colors of the rainbow affect people's senses in different ways. To me, blue is like ice, or a deep pool of water, or cool air from an air conditioner. I would expose the blind person to one of these."

Point #5

Ask for the job!

At the end of each interview, ask: "Do I have the *qualifications to do the job?*" The hiring authority has three options, one of which is "Yes!" If so, follow with, *"When can I start?"*

You can forget about waiting for letters or promised follow-up phone calls – that may never come – from an employer who interviewed you. You'll know how you did before you leave the interview by asking the qualifications question and watching the hiring authority's face.

One response is that you are qualified, but that they have other candidates to see. Fine. Make your final comment something like, "I'm not surprised that you have other candidates, this is a great job opportunity. I'd just like to leave one thought. I want this job! May I call you next Tuesday at 8:30 am, or another convenient time to find out where I stand?"

The interviewer may say, "Since you asked, I don't believe you are suitable for this job." Get the best investment out of your valuable time that you can. Ask the person what it was that they believe you lack, or something you might have said or done during the interview. If you are making a mistake over and over, now is the time to find out.

Begin to think of yourself as a professional crafts person. You have a complete set of skills which you take to any new job. Employers will exchange a paycheck for your skills to reduce costs, increase profits, improve performance or achieve their mission.

The preceding guidance on interviewing and negotiating will ensure that you receive a fair financial offer for the *Advantages* you bring to your career destination.

Who will help you?

Mile 12 is the final stretch of road on your way to a job you'll love. Selecting and preparing your references is critical if you want the career of your dreams. Why? A hiring authority will probably want to talk with your references prior to hiring you. It's up to you to prepare your references for their follow-up phone calls. Explain to your references exactly what the job requires and how your previous *Successes* will meet the needs of your new employer. You may also need to explain the concept of *Items*, *Successes* and *Advantages*. You will certainly want them to mention your *Advantages* in their conversation with your prospective employer.

In over ten years as an executive recruiter, I have had several very sad experiences with candidates losing great career opportunities because of weak or negative reference responses. Many times it is what the reference does *not* say that ends the opportunity. One reference source I checked answered a question about alcohol problems with the response, "You mean *on* the job, right?" As you might imagine, this candidate quickly needed to look for another opportunity with another recruiter. *You'll need three references for each career destination. These will be people who have known you in your professional career.* Good references are essential and you should nurture those contacts through the years. They become particularly valuable if you are not able to use anyone at your present firm.

Professional references for your career destination are:

People who have seen you perform, or can vouch for your character and ability to perform in your next job.

1. Your most recent manager (if possible):

Name_____.

Title_____.

Work telephone_____.

Home telephone_____.

2. A peer who has known you professionally for an extended period of time:

Name_____.

Title_____.

Work telephone_____.

Home telephone_____.

3. A subordinate who has worked for you (if possible):

Name_____.

Title_____.

Work telephone_____.

Home telephone_____.

References *must* be people you trust and who will not reveal the call to anyone at your present job.

Phone your references and mail them a copy of the following form well before a hiring authority calls them. Tell them about the major aspects of the new job and ask them to emphasize the legitimate *Advantages* you bring to the job. *Then ask your references what they will say about you.* If they hesitate in their response, get yourself another reference! Prepare your reference with the following information:

Send the information to each professional reference *prior to their contact with your prospective employer.*

"Thanks for supporting me by talking to:

_____

(Name of person who you will be calling) *who works for:*_____ (Employer name).
If you miss the call, they can be reached at:

_____

The opportunity I am interested in is:

_____
(Title)

_____
(Location)

They will be asking me to:

1._____.

2._____.

3._____.

I'd be delighted to have you share your feelings or experiences that support what I have to offer this position. My three Advantages that match this job are:

1._____.

2._____.

3._____.

Please give me a call once you've been contacted. I'm really excited about this job; I'll give you a call to find out how things went. Thanks for your help."

Once you've heard from your reference, *immediately* send them a sincere thank you note for their assistance.

Appendix

<u>Mile</u> specific Helpful Hints to speed you on your way to a great job!

Here are examples you may find useful in specific <u>Miles</u>. These are actual examples taken from the author's journey.

Helpful Hints for <u>Mile 02</u>
See *your* map to the future!

(Refer to page 17.)

Bill Karlson's work personality preferences:

- **I prefer to recharge by myself**
- **I prefer expressing thoughts by talking**
- **I prefer to discuss one topic at a time**
- **I am more reliant on facts than theory**
- **I make decisions on logic**
- **I make important decisions independently**
- **I like scheduled and predictable work**
- **I prefer things as they are.**

1. *Job management preferences:*

Would like a manager who gives clear direction, leaves me alone to complete my job, checks periodically on progress and gives supportive feedback.

2. *General preferred work activities:*

- **Directing others**
- **Some written work**
- **Presenting ideas and results to a group**
- **Solving problems using a computer**

3. *Preferred work environment would include:*

- **Spending most time indoors**
- **Like an opportunity for fresh air**
- **A well lighted, window office**
- **The chance to move around independently**
- **Periodic interaction with work peers**
- **One that emphasizes ethical values and the importance of family**

4. *The most attractive organizational structure:*

- **Well funded, with low debt**
- **50+ employees – less than 300 at site**

5. *Preferred relationship with employer management:*

Where I have the ability to be in on things, part of the decision making process which results in meaningful change.

6. *Preferred relationship with peers:*

Easy going, supportive, with a "we're in this together" attitude.

7. *If supervisory management is a part of my job:*

I'd like the chance to understand their personalities, learn how they would like to be managed, set specific goals, and manage against these objectives while giving my people a chance to grow and expand their contribution.

8. *Continuing professional development:*

The financial and time support from my employer to continue to learn and expand my contribution beyond my immediate job description. This would include purchase of software, tapes, books and the ability to attend seminars.

9. *Equipment support:*

The most current computer equipment, access to the Internet, mobile phone, home telephone line and support equipment.

10. *Physical work environment:*

Prefer a space away from routine foot traffic that allows me to limit access and minimize distractions.

Five sample questions Bill must have answered in choosing career titles and before accepting an opportunity.

1. How will I be managed?

2. What opportunities will I have to express my opinion (and at what cost)?

3. How much freedom will I have to set my own agenda in conjunction with the employer's objectives?

4. **What opportunities will I have to advance, either through promotion or increased income?**

5. **What is the employer's stability or my job security?**

Helpful Hints for <u>Mile 03</u>
What you have to offer!

(Refer to pages 24 and 25.)

Other excellent resources are Richard Nelson Bolles'
What Color Is Your Parachute? and Bernard Hal-
dane's *Career Satisfaction and Success: A Guide to
Job and Personal Freedom.*

Stories, strengths, and areas to avoid

Cheryl's story

"It all started with a vision. In early 1991, I realized
my parents would be celebrating their fiftieth wedding anniversary February 1, 1992. From that moment on I had a vision of Mother and Dad dancing to
'their song:' a 40's tune called *Honey.* The vision, as
well as the song, kept running through my head. I
decided to have a reception for family and friends but
wanted to surprise the folks. This would be hard as
many friends live in Knoxville. (I live in Nashville,
200 miles away.) I met with my brother to be sure he
was in agreement. Next I decided to have the party at
a local hotel to accommodate the many out-of-town-
ers and set my budget. I planned several tasks:

    1. Obtained rates from hotels: rooms and
       catering;
    2. Called out-of-town people to mark their
       calendars;
    3. Ordered invitations;
    4. Lined up florist;
    5. Contacted calligrapher;

6. Bought mother's dress which we gave to her Christmas of 1991 with a poem saying we were taking them out for their anniversary;
7. Decided on the menu and ordered the wedding cake;
8. To cut costs I used several of the young people who were very knowledgeable to video the party as well as take still photos;
9. I was able to find a 4-piece band composed of a group of retired folk who knew the 40's tunes. They even learned the song: *Honey* just for this event.

The reception was a great success. Mother and Dad were surprised and delighted."

Cheryl's strengths

• Able to clearly visualize a future event and use it to drive tasks to support the goal.
• Able to use imagination to create an enjoyable experience for all.
• Clear written and oral communication skills; able to get my point across clearly and quickly; able to communicate from out-of-town.
• Worked well within a defined time frame.
• Built good working relationships with all the vendors. Negotiated arrangements.
• Comparison shopped; made good use of money.
• Able to prioritize and stay focused.

Cheryl's areas to avoid

"Negotiating; I do not like to negotiate even though I am good at it."

Harry's stories

1. "I am in my second career now. I am responsible for product development, marketing and selling my company's career products and services. One market segment is managers, professionals and technical types in career change or job search. I feel good about the sale I made to a state government department that helps dislocated workers get back to work. I downloaded a list of contacts in the fifty states from the U.S. Department of Labor's Web Page and telephoned state officials to learn their needs and introduced *GET TOP $$$ IN A JOB YOU LOVE!* Through telephone and hardcopy presentations and discussions, describing how this career achievement and job search book will speed up placement of dislocated workers, the state sent a purchase order."

2. "An unemployed professional in the printing industry asked for help to overcome his problem during interviews with hiring authorities. He had difficulty explaining why he was fired from his last (six month) job at a public higher education institution. His previous job of ten years was with a rapidly expanding, highly entrepreneurial company – which went out of business due to lack of capital. I knew the high quality of both organizations. After understanding the situation, I observed that while he had thrived in one corporate culture, he had not survived the second. Hence, I suggested he seek out employers with a entrepreneurial style work environment in which he can again thrive and also that he explain to future hiring authorities he had simply made a mistake in his decision to work with the last organization which had a culture that was not a good match with who he is and his preferred work style."

3. "In my former 35-year public service career in state and federal government I was responsible for marketing technical services to local economic development organizations and small and medium size manufacturers to help solve problems in their economic growth. I had to learn about many services and how they could be used, build working relationships with community and state groups, identify needs, arrange services from different sources, and coordinate the delivery. I feel good about the many communities and manufacturers my efforts helped."

4. "I was the first American national to participate in the Graduate Program in Economic Development, Vanderbilt University, leading to a master's degree in economics. This is a program designed for lower and mid level professionals in governments from around the world to upgrade their skills in economic growth."

5. "I built a 6-foot long slanted shelf shoe rack for my wife's closet. I conceived what it would look like, how it could be built and with what materials. I bought and cut the wood, assembled it with wood screws, primed and painted it. She was pleased. It looks good and works well."

6. "I was one of four co-founders of the Middle Tennessee Chapter of the Association for Quality and Participation. We created a forum for government, non-profit organization, and company managers and employees to upgrade skills in facilitating quality improvement through employee involvement."

Harry's strengths

• Can make things happen. (The name of the game: identify an opportunity and find a way to make it a reality).
• Can develop market nichés and close sales.
• Thrives in a multi-cultural work environment.
• Can invent solutions to work problems after a quick yet thorough analysis
• Can listen with empathy and understanding to a person's situation and offer alternatives and other resources to meet needs.
• Can build long-term alliances to reach and serve customers.
• Can innovate improvements in products/services.
• Has great respect for and interest in others and their abilities; likes to encourage.
• Thrives in a close working relationship with supervisor or mentor, with frequent daily contact for input and feedback in striving for shared goals.

Harry's areas to avoid

"Situations where I do not have quick and ready access to other team members."

Items

Examples of Bill's *Items* that have been matched to a career path which will be used to support each career choice résumé:

1. *Career Achievement Speaker*

1 Recorded professional speaker.
1 Nationally Certified Personnel Consultant.
1 Responsible for training and contract negotiation.
1 Other challenging jobs 1973-78.
1 Lions Club Tail Twister, United Way Director.
1 Published professional writer and recorded public speaker.
1 Bachelor of Science in Business Administration, University of Delaware.
1 Field engineer from 1978-82.

2. *Industrial Sales Professional*

2 Professional speaker at job fair sponsored by CNBC.
2 Recorded professional speaker.
2 Nationally Certified Personnel Consultant.
2 Reduced costs and increased earnings on a multi-million dollar business.
2 Responsible for training and contract negotiation.
2 Introduced and increased sales of high performance coatings in the western U.S. and Far East with long term Fortune 500 accounts.
2 Field engineer from 1978-82.
2 Other challenging jobs with the DuPont Company from 1973-78.
2 Lions Club Tail Twister, United Way Director.
2 Published writer and recorded public speaker.

2 Bachelor of Science in Business Administration, University of Delaware.

3. *Corrosion Coatings Specialist*

3 Responsible for Ford and General Motors site coatings accounts.

3 Field and laboratory trained in corrosion theory and application methods.

3 Responsible for management, training and contract negotiation.

3 Coatings field engineer from 1978-82.

3 Other challenging jobs 1973-78.

3 National Association of Corrosion Engineers certification.

3 Bachelor of Science in Business Administration, University of Delaware.

Successes

Bill Karlson's career title matched *Successes* based on previous *Items* and other life experiences.

Successes to build on *Items*:

1. *Career Achievement Speaker*

1 Successful seminar speaker for New York job fair, sponsored by CNBC.

1 Author of the successful *GET TOP $$$ IN A JOB YOU LOVE!*sм series.

1 Top Producer in the state engineering recruiting competition.

1 Rookie of the Year, starting with no accounts.

1 Reduced costs/increased sales on multimillion dollar business.

1 Directed engineering staff on profitable high performance coatings maintenance contracts.
1 Introduced and increased sales of high performance coatings in the western U.S. and Far East with long-term Fortune 500 accounts.

2. Industrial Sales Professional

2 Successful seminar speaker for New York job fair.
2 Author of the successful *GET TOP $$$ IN A JOB YOU <u>LOVE</u>!*
2 Top Producer in the state engineering recruiting competition.
2 Office Rookie of the Year, starting with no accounts in a new market.
2 Planned and conducted successful technical education seminars for Fortune 500 companies. Strong audience response, exceptional interest generated.
2 Directed engineering staff on profitable high performance coatings maintenance contracts.

3. Corrosion Coatings Specialist

3 Rookie of the year for this site in the chemical and corrosion coatings industry.
3 Managed high dollar accounts while successfully introducing new high performance products.
3 Reduced costs and increased earnings on a multi-million dollar maintenance coatings business.
3 Directed engineering staff on profitable high performance coatings maintenance contracts.
3 Introduced and increased sales of high performance coatings in the western U.S. and Far East.
3 DuPont Hard Hat Award for two years in a row for outstanding performance as a field engineer.

Three key job-specific performance elements

After choosing three career destinations, Bill had to find at least three key things that would ensure him getting a job he loved. These key job-specific performance elements were obtained from experience as well as from talking to those already in the industry using the suggested script in Mile 06. They will be used on each of Bill's three résumés.

1. Career Achievement Speakers must:

   a. Be exciting and present a professional image in front of audiences.
   b. Possess excellent communications skills.
   c. Present a compelling argument for positive career change.

2. Industrial Sales Professionals have to:

   a. Show profitability gains through communication.
   b. Make an excellent first impression on clients.
   c. Achieve profitability goals.

3. Corrosion Coatings Specialists must be able to:

   a. Quickly determine cause and effect.
   b. Have strong knowledge of corrosion coatings.
   c. Estimate square footage and successfully negotiate contracts.

Helpful Hints for <u>Mile 06</u>
Other exciting career destinations!

Bill's career destinations

Bill will be most effective by choosing an ideal career that closely matches the preceding answers from <u>Mile 05</u>. After careful reflection, Bill's ideal career job is to become a nationally-recognized career achievement speaker, a dream he has had for many years.

He has chosen a second job option in industrial sales, and a third as a corrosion coatings specialist, based on previous job experience and potential job fulfillment.

1. Career Achievement Speaker
2. Industrial Sales Professional
3. Corrosion Coatings Specialist

Helpful Hints for <u>Mile 08</u>
World's most powerful résumé!

The *Advantage-Driven Résumé*

Use the *Items, Successes,* and *Advantages (ISAs)* you prepared in <u>Miles 03</u> and <u>08</u> as the basis for developing each of your résumés. You do not have to use exactly what you prepared. It should be used to generate ideas to prepare exceptionally powerful résumés.

Take a look at the three following *ISAs* and resulting résumés for Bill Karlson. You'll see that each is specifically geared to Bill's chosen ideal, second and third career paths. *Within ten seconds of quick review, each résumé provides solutions to problems a future employer needs to be solved. These are highlighted by using a future tense worded (can, will) Advantage, supported by a previous Success and given credibility with an Item. Believe me, these are the résumés that hiring authorities put in the "TO BE CALLED" short stack.*

Ideal career path:

1. Career Achievement Speaker

Items to support *Successes* and *Advantages* on Bill's résumé to be hired as Career Achievement Speaker:

Items (previous and present facts)

1 Recorded professional speaker.
1 Nationally Certified Personnel Consultant.
1 Responsible for training and contract negotiation.
1 Other challenging jobs 1973-78.
1 Lions Club, United Way Director.
1 Published professional writer and recorded public speaker.
1 Bachelor of Science in Business Administration, University of Delaware.
1 Field engineer from 1978-82.

Successes to build on *Items* and give *Advantages* credibility

1 Successful seminar speaker for New York job fair, sponsored by CNBC.
1 Author of *GET TOP $$$ IN A JOB YOU LOVE!* book, seminars and radio show
1 Top Producer in the state engineering recruiting competition.
1 Office Rookie of the Year, starting with no accounts in a new market.
1 Reduced costs and increased earnings in a multimillion dollar business.

1 Directed engineering staff on profitable high performance coatings maintenance contracts.
1 Introduced and increased sales of high performance coatings in the western U.S. and Far East with long term Fortune 500 accounts.

Advantages to support being hired as a professional Career Achievement Speaker

1 Will present an exciting and professional image to your audience.
1 Will bring exceptional communications and interpersonal skills to career achievement.
1 Through unique approaches can increase sales to achieve substantial gains.
1 Can positively affect audiences to want to proceed with their own career achievement.
1 Can achieve profit goals.
1 Can successfully maintain long term sales relationships.

Bill Karlson

P.O. Box 1423, Brentwood, TN 37024-1423

Message (615) 259-7711

Pager (615) 200-8007

President, World Career Achievement Company   **1994-now**

• **Will present an exciting and professional image to your audience.** Successful seminar speaker for New York job fair. Sponsored by CNBC. Skilled radio talk show host.

President, Karlson Associates, International   **1989-1994**

• **Will bring exceptional communications and interpersonal skills to career achievement.** Author, *GET TOP $$$ IN A JOB YOU LOVE!* Top recruiting producer. Nationally Certified Personnel Consultant.

Account Executive, Management Recruiters International   **1987-1989**

• **Through unique approaches can increase sales to achieve substantial gains.** Rookie of the Year, starting with no accounts in a new market.

Account Manager, DuPont Company (1973-1987)   **1986-1986**

• **Can positively affect audiences to want to proceed with their own career achievement.** Planned and conducted successful technical education seminars for Fortune 500 companies. Strong audience response, exceptional interest generated.

Operations Manager, DuPont Company   **1983-1986**

• **Can achieve profit goals.** Reduced costs and increased earnings on a multimillion dollar business. Directed engineering staff on profitable high performance coatings maintenance contracts. Responsible for training and contract negotiation.

Senior Sales Representative, DuPont Company   **1982-1983**

• **Can successfully maintain long term sales relationships.** Introduced and increased sales of high performance coatings in the western U.S. and Far East with long term Fortune 500 accounts. Field engineer from 1978-82. Other challenging jobs 1973-78.

Outside Success

• Lions Club Tail Twister, United Way Division Director
• Published professional writer and recorded public speaker

Education

• Bachelor of Science in Business Administration, University of Delaware

Second career path:

2. Industrial Sales Professional

Items to support *Successes* and *Advantages* to be hired as an Industrial Sales Professional:

Items (previous and present facts)

2 **Professional speaker at job fair sponsored by CNBC.**
2 **Recorded professional speaker.**
2 **Nationally Certified Personnel Consultant.**
2 **Reduced costs and increased earnings on a multimillion dollar business.**
2 **Responsible for training and contract negotiation.**
2 **Introduced and increased sales of high performance coatings in the western U.S. and Far East basin with long term Fortune 500 accounts.**
2 **Field engineer from 1978-82.**
2 **Other challenging jobs with the DuPont Company - 1973-78.**
2 **Lions Club Tail Twister, United Way Division Director.**
2 **Published professional writer and recorded public speaker.**
2 **Bachelor of Science in Business Administration, University of Delaware.**

Successes to build on *Items* and give *Advantages* credibility

2 **Successful seminar speaker for New York job fair.**
2 **Author of successful** *GET TOP $$$ IN A JOB YOU <u>LOVE</u>!sm* **programs, seminars and radio show.**
2 **Top Producer in the state engineering recruiting competition.**
2 **Office Rookie of the Year, starting with no accounts in a new market.**
2 **Planned and conducted successful technical education seminars for Fortune 500 companies. Strong audience response, exceptional interest generated.**
2 **Directed engineering staff on profitable high performance coatings maintenance contracts.**

Advantages to support being hired as a professional in Industrial Sales

2 **Can achieve dramatic profitability gains through communications skills.**
2 **Bring exceptional communications and interpersonal skills to challenging situations.**
2 **Through unique approaches can increase sales to achieve substantial sales gains.**
2 **Will make an excellent first impression on top clients.**
2 **Can achieve profit goals.**
2 **Can successfully maintain long-term sales relationships.**

Bill Karlson

P.O. Box 1423, Brentwood, TN 37024-1423
Message (615) 259-7711

Pager (615) 200-8007

Chief Operating Officer, NiS International   **1994-now**

• **Can achieve dramatic profitability gains through communications skills.** Substantially increased cash flow through copyrighted human resources profiling and job matching system. Author, *GET TOP $$$ IN A JOB YOU LOVE!*, which continues to generate repeat income.

President, Karlson Associates, International   **1989-1994**

• **Bring exceptional communications and interpersonal skills to challenging situations.** Top Producer. Nationally Certified Personnel Consultant.

Account Executive, Management Recruiters International   **1987-1989**

• **Through unique approaches can increase sales to achieve substantial sales gains.** Office Rookie of the Year for this site.

Account Manager, DuPont Company (1973-1987)   **1986-1986**

• **Will make an excellent first impression on top clients.** Managed accounts while successfully introducing new high performance products.

Operations Manager, DuPont Company   **1983-1986**

• **Can achieve profit goals.** Reduced costs and increased earnings on a mul timillion dollar business. Directed engineering staff on profitable high performance coatings maintenance contracts. Responsible for training and contract negotiation.

Senior Sales Representative, DuPont Company   **1982-1983**

• **Can successfully maintain long term sales relationships.** Introduced and increased sales of high performance coatings in the western U.S. and Far East. Field engineer from 1978-82. Other challenging jobs 1973-78.

Outside Success

• Board of Directors - United Cerebral Palsy
• Published professional writer and recorded public speaker
• Professional snow skiing instructor

Education

• Bachelor of Science in Business Administration, University of Delaware

Third career path:

3. Corrosion Coatings Specialist

Items to support *Successes* and *Advantages* on Bill's résumé to be hired as Corrosion Coatings Specialist:

Items (previous and present facts)

3 **Responsible for Ford and General Motors site accounts.**
3 **Field and laboratory trained in corrosion theory and application methods.**
3 **Responsible for management, training and contract negotiation.**
3 **Coatings field engineer from 1978-82.**
3 **National Association of Corrosion Engineers course certification.**
3 **Bachelor of Science in Business Administration, University of Delaware.**

Successes to build on *Items* and give *Advantages* credibility

3 **Rookie of the Year for this site in the chemical and corrosion coatings industry.**
3 **Managed high dollar accounts while successfully introducing new high performance products.**
3 **Reduced costs and increased earnings on a multimillion dollar maintenance coatings business.**
3 **Directed engineering staff on profitable high performance coatings maintenance contracts.**

performance coatings in the western U.S.
and Far East.
3 **DuPont Hard Hat Award (twice) for out
standing performance as a field coatings
engineer.**

Advantages to support being hired as a professional
Corrosion Coatings Specialist:

3 **Can achieve profitability gains through
field communications skills.**
3 **Bring exceptional communications and
interpersonal skills to challenging field
situations.**
3 **Through unique approaches can increase
field sales to achieve substantial sales
gains.**
3 **Will make an excellent first impression on
top clients.**
3 **Can achieve profit goals.**
3 **Can quickly determine cause and effect.**
3 **Can successfully maintain long term sales
relationships.**
3 **Will accurately estimate square footage
and successfully negotiate contracts.**

Bill   Karlson

P.O. Box 1423, Brentwood, TN 37024-1423

Message (615) 259-7711

Pager   (615)   200-8007

Director, Executive Search Division, NiS   **1994-now**

• **Can achieve dramatic profitability gains through field communications skills.** Top financial producer in the chemical engineering division of my state. Million dollar circle award.

President, Karlson Associates, International   **1989-1994**

• **Bring exceptional communications and interpersonal skills to challenging field situations.** Able to communicate effectively with all levels of engineering management. Quickly analyzed technical job performance criteria and diverse chemical engineering recruiting assignments.

Account Executive, Management Recruiters International   **1987-1989**

• **Through unique approaches can increase field sales to achieve substantial sales gains.** Office Rookie of the year for this site in the chemical and corrosion coatings industry.

Account Manager, DuPont Company (1973-1987)   **1986-1986**

• **Will make an excellent first impression on top clients.** Managed high dollar accounts while successfully introducing new high performance products. Responsible for Ford and General Motors site accounts. Field and laboratory trained in corrosion theory and application methods.

Operations Manager, DuPont Company   **1983-1986**

• **Can quickly determine cause and effect.** Reduced costs and increased earnings on a multimillion dollar maintenance coatings business. Managed engineering staff on high performance coatings maintenance contracts.

Senior Sales Representative, DuPont Company   **1982-1983**

• **Can successfully maintain long term sales relationships.** Introduced and increased sales of high performance coatings in western U.S./Far East.

Field Engineer, DuPont Company   **1978-1982**

• **Will accurately estimate square footage and successfully negotiate contracts.** Possess knowledge of coatings. National Association of Corrosion Engineers class certification.

Education

• Bachelor of Science in Business Administration, University of Delaware

Helpful Hints for <u>Mile 11</u>
Going for top starting salary!

How to resign from your current job.

Let's look at the potentially difficult challenge of leaving a job where you have made a contribution and are well accepted. Once you've received that terrific offer in writing, we recommend resigning in writing. The following is a sample resignation letter:

Date

Dear (current boss' name),

I respectfully resign my position of (current title) from (current employer's name), effective (two weeks from the resignation date).

Desiring to continue my career growth and development, I've accepted a position with (new employer's name and the location). My career with the organization begins on (new start date).

My experiences with (current employer) have been very rewarding and I appreciate all of the opportunities I've been given. I will look back on my time here as very positive and will miss the many fine friends I've made.

Respectfully,

your signature

(Some people forget to sign.)

Cognitive dissonance (buyer's remorse)

So now that you've arrived at your new career (having submitted your resignation to your old firm), please realize that changing your job can be very stressful for you, your spouse and others. Since you've been doing a good job, your employer may not want to lose you.

You may get a counter offer, even though you've accepted another job and resigned. It may be tough for you to walk away from a job that has had its great times. You are going to miss friends you've made. Being made a counter offer can be a terrific experience. You may be tempted to stay. Don't get emotional and lose sight of why you looked for another job in the first place.

Cognitive dissonance, similar to buyer's remorse, can cause you to emotionally negate your first positive decision and stay on with your old firm.

Your next career destination should be selected without emotional tangents. People close to you may try to influence you. You know things aren't right at your current job. Your current job may not get any better. It's up to you to end your relationship professionally. Two weeks notice is the industry standard.

How much time would you be given in a layoff or take-over situation? The paternalistic patterns of the past are gone forever. There's now a corporate focus on the bottom line. You may have a reaction to the stress of resigning. You may question your decision after it has been made. This is normal. It's an expected feeling that many candidates experience. The following pointers on examining counter offers may help you through the first few days of the stress from *resigning*.

Consider all the reasons for pursuing a great new career opportunity in the first place. Before accepting a counter offer, consider where the money for the counter offer is coming from. Is it your next pay raise early? All companies have relatively inflexible wage and salary guidelines they must follow.

What type of employer would wait until you submitted your resignation before he would give you a raise anyway? Your employer may keep an eye out for a new person at a lower salary to replace you, even after you've accepted their counter offer. From this day on, your loyalty may be in question. Promotion opportunities might decrease or disappear altogether, based upon the employer's perception of your loyalty.

When raises are tougher to come by, your employer might begin cutbacks with you. Everything that caused you to consider a change at first will probably still be there in the future, even after you accept the counter offer. Do you really think things will change and you'll be made happy? Statistics show that if you accept a counter offer, the probability of you voluntarily leaving within six months, or being let go within one year, is significantly higher than if you never told them you were looking. Accepting a counter offer could be an insult to your intelligence and a blow to your pride, if you later begin to sense that you were "bought" by the old employer.

Once the word gets out that you submitted your resignation, but accepted the employer's counter offer, the relationship that you've enjoyed with co-workers might change. You could lose the personal satisfaction of peer group acceptance, if they sense management may be watching who is friendly with whom. Being on the right team is important to future promotions.

Carefully think through your present employer's counter offer, after receiving a written offer from another firm. You should have a much better understanding of who you are, what you can offer, and what it takes to make you happy at your career destination.

Sample response to want ads

(Return to page 66, end of first paragraph)

Because the odds are so low for success in sending your résumé in to a want ad, we would really like to see you avoid the pain of rejection. However, we know that hope springs eternal, and after all, they have to hire *somebody*.

Try to find out who ran the ad. This includes knowing the company and name of the hiring authority (typically *not* the name listed in the ad). For blind ads to post office boxes, call the area post office and they will tell you who ran the ad. Avoid the embarrassment of sending your résumé in to your own company! Call the company and get a hiring authority's name, or at least the person who manages the human resource department.

Your cover letter should be *no more than two paragraphs long*. Ignore any requests for salary. Cut out the ad and attach it to your cover letter/résumé. You'd be surprised at how confusing it can be in trying to match a résumé to a job opening. Sample:

Dear _____:

I am sending you my résumé in response to your ad for a _____ (job title) which ran in the _____ paper on ____ (date it ran). A copy of the ad is attached.

I'll give you a call on _____ (date) at ____ (time) to discuss how you feel I meet _____'s (company name) needs. Or call me at _____.

Sincerely,

Your signature

Index

Accepting an offer, 93,96,97
Advantage-Driven Résumésм,
   9,23,26,65,70,73,126,129,132
Advantages, 9,23,61,67,68,69,125,128,131
Alternative career paths (job titles), 42,45
Areas to avoid (weaknesses), 25,114,117
Ask for the job, 96,102
Bates, Marilyn, 19
Benefit package, 98
Bolles, Richard Nelson, 113
Career change trauma, 8
Career destinations, 40,42,122
Career passion, 7,10,11,16,32,40,42,62,79,82,88
Career title, 40,44,45,68
Compensation package, 98
Cover letters, 72,137
Covey, Stephen, R., 86
Dream career, 10,24,32,40,45,76
Employer's culture, 19,115
Employer research, 11,49
Executive recruiters, 12,51,75
Focus, 10,11,38,63
Goal achievement planning, 29,86
      Career, 32
      Community, 34
      Family, 35
      Financial, 35
      Mental, 36
      Physical, 36
      Social, 37
      Spiritual, 38
"Golden handcuffs," 16
Haldane, Bernard, 24,84,113

NOTES

_____

_____

_____

_____

_____

_____

_____

_____

_____

_____

_____

_____

_____

NOTES

_____

_____

_____

_____

_____

_____

_____

_____

_____

_____

_____

_____

_____

NOTES

_____

_____

_____

_____

_____

_____

_____

_____

_____

_____

_____

_____

_____

I'd be delighted to hear from you! Please write and tell me how the approaches and techniques worked for you. I read every letter sent to me.

Bill Karlson

Bill Karlson
GT$ 3rd Edition
P.O. Box 681666
Franklin, TN 37068

We also have job search and career achievement tapes, a formal step-by-step guidebook and in-person seminar dates available for you or your group.

Please *call* (800) 259-7711 for more information.

Thanks for your support!